Sanders   385
Brasspounder   S
                27578

3 1614 00018 2932

SEP 6 78

Sanders   385
Brasspounder   S
                27578

MIDLOTHIAN PUBLIC LIBRARY

Midlothian
Public Library

14701 S. Kenton Ave.
Midlothian, IL 60445

1. be

2. y for
   ooks
   such

3. ooks

4. or

THE BRASSPOUNDER

THE BRASSPOUNDER

D. G. SANDERS

HAWTHORN BOOKS, INC.
Publishers / New York
A Howard & Wyndham Company

385
S

THE BRASSPOUNDER

Library of Congress Catalog Card Number: 77-072820

ISBN: 0-8015-0881-9

1 2 3 4 5 6 7 8 9 10

To Irene, Jane, and Sandra

Contents

Introduction

This is the story of how it used to be in the romantic days of railroading—when railroads were run by railroad people and not by the moneylenders. When the entire force, from the policymaker at the top to the track laborer at the bottom, took pride in a railroad's service, its efficiency, its safety, and its personal appearance. When engines were wiped and brass was polished and the paint gang worked the year around. When symmetrical white stone lines marked the borders of hundreds of miles of main track and not a weed was allowed to grow in the sixfoot. When station after station maintained a trim flower and shrubbery garden near its door. When no one believed that one day the country's prestigious Blue Ribbon fleet would be referred to editorially as a "faded splendor," and that pride and enthusiasm would be replaced by shame and excuse.

When "safety first" was not just a catchword, to be preached and practiced only when it cost nothing. When this slogan was symbolized by the lonely trackwalker who patrolled the main line by night with his toolbag, his spike maul, and his lantern. When esteem was contagious and promoted itself; when "on time" was a religion. When engineers gained enviable reputations and strove to live up to them. When these same understood, individually, the steam engines they handled—their capabilities and their weaknesses, how to pamper and get the utmost out of each—and, in the process, developed a quite obvious fondness for them.

A time when the brasspounder took a great pride in his unique profession and in the knowledge that he was the railroad's nervous system. A time when he was immensely proud to be a member of a great team that moved his country's commerce. A time before the expedient came to supersede the rule. A time when so many things were personal, and where everything would eventually become impersonal.

It was 1915 and a time when nobody, from the railroad president down to the water boy, had any idea that railroad employment was within a few years of reaching its peak. The boom, we thought, would go on forever—what else? As our country grew, its railroads would have to grow in proportion in order to haul its people and their goods.

That's what we thought in 1915—if, indeed, we thought at all.

THE BRASSPOUNDER

A Barefoot Boy

I was born in 1899 in the village of Hemlock, which lay among the hills and coal mines of Perry County, Ohio. Hemlock had a few hundred people and three churches that didn't interrelate much. It had one saloon and a poolroom that were more democratic. There was one level street, a few hundred feet long and unpaved, on which were located the business places and some houses. One of these was a well-kept old home fronted by a level expanse of lawn, in a corner of which stood a huge willow.

Now nobody with any sense of fitness would choose a willow tree to decorate his lawn. They are altogether unsuitable, being litterbugs, and their slender leaves provide spotty shade.

But the willow had not been chosen for this site. It had been planted quite by accident. The place had belonged to a young Civil War cavalryman by the name of Stallsmith. Home on a short leave, he had dismounted from his horse and stuck his riding switch into the ground. He rode away again without taking it. Later, his family noted that it was sprouting leaf buds. By the turn of the century it had become the big willow that I remember.

Our streets had no names and the roads about had no numbers. The hills around us, however, were all named, and this served quite as well when a reference point was needed. We had Bohemian Heights, Honey Hill, Dugan Ridge, and Whippstown Ridge. Three miles to the east of us was Millertown Hill, on which the Confederate raider John Hunt Morgan and his small army had once encamped for the night, along with four of Grandfather Sanders' best horses.

Grandfather had followed, at a discreet distance. And two days later, when Union troops disbanded the raiders in the woods near Salineville, up in Columbiana County—capturing Morgan in the process—Grandpa went forward, identified his animals, and led them back home.

It may be noted that Sunday Creek ran through our middle, and forever had a rusty red bottom, due to the copper as water pumped into it by several mines along its course. It had no fish, but harbored some frogs and muskrats.

The Z&W railroad ran along the edge of town. Z&W stood for Zanesville & Western, officially—or Zigzag & Wobble, unofficially. I thought it a marvelous little railroad and I didn't care much for this aspersion. But later I would hear other railroads belittled for no better reason—such as "Delay, Linger, and Wait" for the Delaware, Lackawanna & Western," and "Walk and Leave Early" for the Wheeling & Lake Erie.

I was a great string saver in those days. Stores used a lot of it. Few foods were prepackaged then. Crackers, sugar, and pickles were sold from barrels; dried fruits from a

At home in Hemlock, Ohio, in 1912

wooden box; beans from a huge cotton bag. I saved string with a purpose. Bit by bit, pieces were tied together and wrapped around a stick. I resented it when somebody wanted to borrow a piece. However, by the time spring came around, I would have a roll big enough for my purpose. My purpose was to make a baseball.

You began with the biggest cork you could find, whittling this as nearly round as possible. Then began the task of winding—a work of love. You kept the string tight and bore in mind that it was a sphere you were forming.

Lastly, you borrowed your mother's biggest darning needle and began the stitching and knotting, knotting and stitching, until you were completely satisfied with a neat job that wouldn't ravel. You ended up with a sense of accomplishment—and a very usable ball. It was called a "corden" ball, inasmuch as it was made of cord and had no cover. It carried quite well when batted, and I'm sure it was more valued than if it had been bought.

But we didn't live entirely in the dark ages at this time. The town boasted two Model T automobiles—the term *horseless carriage* by now virtually having been dropped.

Moreover, the Secrest family had come into possession of the first phonograph in our midst—yes, a phonograph—a real status symbol of the time. But it wasn't known by that name. People called it the *talking machine*. It, along with its four or five cylindrical records, were made by the Edison Company—a fact proclaimed at the conclusion of each record.

The machine had a long tin horn, modeled after the morning glory. At it's side was a crank, which had to be periodically turned to rewind the interior spring that powered the thing.

Of course, this machine sang as well as talked, but it didn't perform either function too clearly. It had quite a scratchy voice and its words often had to be guessed at. However, if a song was one that was familiar to the listener, the indistinct words could be supplied. But it came about that a line in one song was to raise debate—debate and dissention as to its words. A replay of the record did nothing to resolve this difference. This line seemed to be either:

Rocked in the cradle of the deep

or

Locked in the stable with the sheep

I was not asked to vote.

The Budding Op

In the spring of 1912, with school out and fancy free, I rather forgot play. I had found a new interest. This was the two clicking telegraph sounders on the three-sided desk in the bay window of our railroad depot. I would make trips downtown just to stand near an open window and listen to them, fascinated. And when Mr. Pierce Osenbaugh, our agent-operator sat at this desk and wrote down something that one of them said to him, replying with his fingers, I would be carried away in gaping wonder.

Now be it noted that in that day telegraphers were a special kind of people. They were thought to be especially talented and their advice was sought. They got notices in the paper now and then, and fables were attached to some. There was one fabulous fellow, never named, who could send a message with one hand while taking down another message with the other hand. This account had a discouraging effect on me at the time I heard it. I was sure I could never attain to that degree of proficiency. I was a long time in realizing that such a person never was.

The Z&W operated an early morning passenger train, from Shawnee to Zanesville, that had to use a switchback in order to get up over Manley Hill, just out of Shawnee. It carried many men to work at the Congo mines.

Outside the station there was no bulletin board that announced the time of this train, nor of its afternoon counterpart in other direction. The departure time of the morning train was of importance to many people, and some miner, with view of performing a public service, had written on the station's nicely painted front: "DINKY DUE 6:17."

It was a crude inscription. His writing instrument had been the oily black wick of his miner's lamp. Pierce didn't appreciate this, and when I showed up that morning he was trying to wash it off with soap and water, but he wasn't getting anyplace, he only enlarged the smear. By inspiration or by former example, I remember not which, I produced a can of coal oil and rag and cleaned the smudge away quite acceptably. This, it seemed, allowed me to get my foot in the door, and before long I was delighted to find myself at work in the depot with broom and dustrag. Once, I blacked the stove in waiting room.

I haunted the telegraph table and my fascination was no doubt obvious. Then, one glorious never-to-be-forgotten morning Pierce handed me a sheet of paper on which was written, in his own hand, the Morse code—all twenty-six letters and ten numerals. He said, "Why don't you memorize this?" Why don't I! I think I jumped up and down in delight. Then I ran home as fast as I could go and told Ma I was going to be a telegraph operator.

All play was now forgotten. I rose early and retired late and in between did much mumbling to myself as I recited the code —from A to Z and 1 to 0. Then I would choose letters and numerals at random and fit the code to them. I went about my home chores in a daze and sometimes forgot what I was about. When it came time to go berry picking, Ma insistently warned me: "Now don't let that code business run through your head and forget to watch out for snakes."

By the time spring came around again I had advanced a step. I was now entrusted with toting the mail back and forth between station and post office, and with the delivery of an occasional telegram. I always ran both ways on this errand, telegrams being such important things. Too, I was allowed to sit at the telegraph table and "send" with the dead (closed) key, using a newspaper as copy. This was invaluable experience in expressing the memorized code by means of the fingers.

I would learn that each operator as well as each station would be identified by letters, either one or two, known as "sines," the purpose being brevity, of course. Usually, these sine letters were related to the names of individuals or stations. The stations' letters, or letter, were commonly known as the "office call."

One day Pierce, having some work outdoors, seated me at the desk with instructions to listen for the Hemlock office call, which was HK. He said that if I heard this, I was to wait for it to be repeated once, then open the key and holler for him. I had never felt such responsibility befire. I listened avidly to both wires. Then, plain and clear came "HK DI." After a tense moment it was repeated: "HK DI." Upon which I took a step beyond the call of duty as I opened the key and carefully formed the letters, *cmn*, which I had learned was short for *coming*. When Pierce came in I said, "It's the dispatcher." Later, he asked me how I knew it was the dispatcher who had called. I said, "He sined DI." And Pierce's eye twinkled.

I now keenly felt the need of a practice set, and had been drooling over those shown in our Sears Roebuck catalog. They were pictured in black and white, of course, but my imagination supplied the sparkle and shine. There were three choices to be had, but the cost of the cheapest was dismaying. Minus battery, but with postage added, this was a bit over five dollars, and I didn't have five cents. Moreover, school was soon to open again and I knew Ma had been scraping money together to buy me some clothing, so I didn't mention practice set at home.

Then one glorious day there was a change in the wind, and before it was over I had a job—that is, a paying job.

A small new mine had opened near our home. They were ready to begin operations and had brought in two horses. The owner that day had approached my father with regard to renting our barn, which had four stalls. Our cow occupied one, but he would be glad to rent out two of the others.

Hearing of this, a brilliant idea struck me and I was off, without saying a word, to find this mine owner. I hit him up for the job of tending his horses. He asked me, "How much do you want?" I thought of asking a dollar a week, but this sounded like a lot of money, so I said seventy-five cents a week. I said I would feed, water, curry, and harness the horses and clean out the barn. He said, "You're hired." I ran back home, my feet not touching the ground, to sound the great news. I liked horses and liked caring for them, but at the moment the job, to me, meant only a practice telegraph set.

But the course of true love does not run smoothly, and I was to stumble and come near falling down on my job as hostler. The animals worked on a sloppy blue-clay bottom, and they came from the mine with legs and underparts plastered with this. By morning it would have hardened into a clinging crust that could not be curried off without pulling out much hair. They offered objection to this painful ordeal. They hadn't kicked me, but I knew each had entertained the thought. Enough of this. I brought the problem to my father. He said, "Go take charge of them at the mine exit evenings while the clay is wet. Ride one and lead the other up and down the creek a piece." This I did and my problem was no more.

I hoarded every penny of my earnings and added to these when November came by trapping six muskrats along Sunday Creek. These I sold for twenty-five cents apiece, without skinning them.

The carcasses? They were commonly thrown out to dogs or chickens. As hard up as most families of the community were, none would dream of eating a muskrat. Two factors put muskrats way down on the social scale. One was that r-a-t was part of their name; the other was their skinny, hairless tail, which resembled that of the common barn rat. Later in life I would learn from personal experience that they are quite good eating, and considered a delicacy in some quarters, where they may appear on a menu as "marsh rabbit." But there is no accounting for tastes, it is said. Witness the fact that these same folk who disdained the vegetarian muskrat found the also skinny-tailed, carrion-eating 'possum quite acceptable on the table.

Before spring came around once more, I held in my

The practice set

hands an honest-to-goodness telegraph set—perhaps my most prized possession ever. However, it wouldn't function until I got hold of a dry battery. But this was no great problem. It involved only a four-mile walk to Corning, where I'd heard that the telephone company would sell me a used but still serviceable one for a nickel.

I didn't know it then but I was just one of thousands, following the same path in the same manner, while others attended such telegraph schools as Dodge Institute at Valparaiso, Indiana.

For the next year and a half my routine varied only with the seasons. Morse practice and my hostling job, plus as many hours as I could squeeze in at the depot, were of first priority. School, I confess, came last.

The Railroads
and the Telegraph

By 1915 the railroads were tops in their field. They had been challenged by inland canals, especially in Ohio, where much money and effort had been expended on a canal system before and after the Civil War. But where the railroad overtook the canal, there was just no competition and the canal faded.

The basic idea behind the canal was sound enough. There is no cheaper way to move a ton of freight than to float it on water. This holds good for natural waterways, but the canal was something quite else. Its speed was that of the mule that walked the towpath. Its current was sluggish, and it thus tended to fill up with silt, which was costly and time-consuming to dredge out.

The automobile and the truck cast small shadows and made few tracks across the landscape in 1915. As competitors of the railroad, they would be no more a threat than the canal had been, so people believed.

That the airplane might some day develop into yet another competing carrier of passengers and freight was unimaginable. The observation was heard that, "If the Lord had intended man to fly, He would have given him wings, would He not?" And on this premise the airplane was commonly brushed aside.

Just now the American economy in general, and railroads in particular, were entering their greatest boom to date, as we tried our level best to supply the (later *our*) warring European allies with everything in our catalog. If we could make it, raise it, or mine it, it had a market "over there." The railroads must haul all this to the seaboard for transshipment, and that's where I came to fit in—on the ground floor, so to speak.

It was my destiny, then, to join the railroads as a brasspounder—also known in the trade as a telegrapher, a morse man, a wire man, or an op. One succeeded to one of these titles after a few years of apprenticeship during which one was first a tyro and then a ham. During the era of World War I our numbers, here and abroad, were legion. We were probably at our employment peak, and we pretty well maintained this number until the depression years of the early thirties. In later years one of our number was to note: "There used to be quite a herd of us on this continent. Our combined roster once equaled that of the buffalo, and indeed has kept pace as each of us is phased out of the picture."

We had a common patron saint in Samuel F. B. Morse who, way back in 1843, perfected his electromagnetic telegraph, by which man could, for the first time in all his history, make himself heard farther than he could holler or drumbeat. In 1848, by means of a government grant of thirty thousand dollars, an experimental line was stretched from Washington to Baltimore, some forty miles. It worked! It was gloriously successful! But it was much more than that. It was a technological step that in the next hundred years would widen man's horizons beyond his dreams of that day.

In 1858, the first cable was completed across the Atlantic, and Queen Victoria sent President Buchanan the first cablegram.

Historically, wars advance all arts, crafts, and sciences. The Civil War was to greatly improve the use and the function of the telegraph in our country, it was widely employed on both sides in this struggle. President Lincoln's haunting of the Washington telegraph office during the dark days of the war is a dramatic page in American history.

The Railroad Telegrapher

Telegraphers fell into two general categories. The commercial field included a number employed by AT&T, various stock exchanges, and some oil pipelines. The other field was railroad communications, which employed more than all others combined.

As it came to work out, the paths of railroad and of commercial telegraphy came to cross one another in many places. In small towns the railroad station might also be the Western Union outlet. In larger towns, the twenty-four-hour-a-day railroad telegraph office would extend the commercial company's limited office hours.

Such was the case at AL Alliance, Ohio, one night when several students from Mt. Union college came in and waited while one penciled out a telegram home, which was in New Orleans. I read the message back aloud and a young fellow in the background remarked: "How that boy does draw out that Neolins."

Perhaps few patrons ever more appreciated this service than did a brilliant young farm lad and stargazer from along the Auglaize River in Allen County, Ohio. On a snowy night in mid-November 1925, he feverishly and desperately pedaled his bicycle into Delphos, where he dashed up the steps of Pennsylvania Railroad's tower to file a telegram. It was a vital message, addressed to Harvard College Observatory, reporting his discovery, he hoped, of a new comet in the heavens. In professional terms the message detailed the comet's location, magnitude, direction of travel, and speed. On reading the message the operator asked, "Is this some sorta code?" And the lad answered in kind, "Sorta."

Having made the discovery, he must be first to duly report this to the one proper authority for confirmation and recognition. Minutes could make the difference. There would be no second-place honor or award. He was, indeed, first, having beat out a fellow observer over in Poland by six days. He had written his name in the skies. The name is Leslie Peltier.

Much of the foregoing detail is gleaned from his most readable book, *Starlight Nights*, published in 1965. But I recall the news dispatch forty years earlier that recounted his achievement and his humble background, thus exciting my interest and empathy. I never dreamed then that I would one day shake his hand, but this I did, forty years later.

Railroad Technology Advances

Complementing the honorable Mr. Morse's invention of the telegraph, three other great nineteenth-century innovations proved to be a worldwide boost to the railroad industry. The first was the air brake, developed by the American genius, Mr. George Westinghouse, in 1868. This filled a basic need. An engine would move a string of cars and the air brake, also operated by the engineer, would stop them and then release at his command. Equally important is the fact that the air brake always "fails safe."

Another vital advance of this era was the automatic coupler, which replaced the early, dangerous and crippling "link and pin."

Last was the English introduction of Standard, or Greenwich, time to the world at large in 1880. This ingenious idea was contrived primarily with England's far-flung ships in mind. At long last, by this system, the sea captain could confidently log his whereabouts anywhere on the face of the earth.

When the import of this idea was grasped by American railroad management, they descended on Congress en masse in 1883 and demanded a national standard-time law, under which all would operate. Thus they would be able to print and publish intelligible schedules both for the public and for the employees. (Prior to this, "sun time" was the rule, and this was determined by the caprice and fancy of individuals and communities the country over.) Many religious people would not buy the standard time idea. They considered it an encroachment on Divine Law and clung to sun time—unless they wanted to catch a train.

These four ingenious innovations of the nineteenth century proved the pillars on which the railroad industry grew and thrived.

In the mid-1870s, Scottish-born Alexander Graham Bell gave the telephone to us and to the world—that is to say, the feasible *idea* for a telephone. But years would elapse before it became a practical and trustworthy facility that would challenge the telegraph.

It was one thing to send a simple electrical impulse that activated a magnet out over a wire, and quite another to transmit the voice and have it come out intelligibly at the other end. The early bugbear of the telephone was the partial ground, commonly brought about by rain, fog, or even extended periods of humidity. These conditions would twist the voice into a cacophony that "knocked the ear off."

Conversely, these same weather conditions acted to raise the amperage of the simpler morse circuit and bring in the code in a heavier or snappier manner. If the amperage rose too much, all the operator had to do by way of correction was to twist a small thumbscrew a mite to pull the relay's dual magnets a fraction farther away from the oscillating iron finger on which they worked their attraction.

A telephone repairman once asked a complaining customer what the noise on his phone was like. The man said, "It's like six geese and a guinea hen fightin'."

Then there's the story of the village storekeeper who answered his wall phone and, turning to a customer standing by—a henpecked individual of the community—said, "It's for you. I think it's your wife." The man put the receiver awkwardly to his ear and hollered, "Hello!" Just then, lightning struck the line and he was knocked to the floor. Rising shakily to his feet he said, "That's her all right."

We Migrate

The year 1915 was pivotal in my life. At its beginning I was a schoolboy. At its end, I was a young man and a working telegrapher, living far off from my birthplace.

During the winter of 1914-15, my folks reached a long-considered decision. Come March, and school out they would pull up stakes or, more aptly, roots of fifty-odd years, and move up north to Coshocton. It was growing late and the time short in which they might escape a life of static existence. My father had dabbled in life insurance as a sideline to his job as stable boss at Sunday Creek Coal Company's Number Nine Mine, albeit he was a lifelong owner and lover of horses.

The insurance company had offered him a better territory, plus an office. There may have been one other consideration: to insure that I, the youngest of their three sons did not begin his productive years as a miner.

One of my last memories of old Hemlock and the Z&W is the funeral train that passed through town. A personage had died at Shawnee and was to be buried at New Lexington, the county seat. Much of the populace had gathered at

the station to watch this train go through without stopping—
this fact in itself being noteworthy and of much interest. The
distance from Shawnee to New Lexington was no more
than ten miles, but the roads then were axletree-deep in
mud; and hence the special train. The railroad had cooper-
ated by providing engine, baggage car, and coach, each
with evidence of much "spit and polish." The crew had had
some briefing. The whistle was sounded for our crossing in
half tone. The fireman operated the highly polished brass
bell in slow cadence. The wide baggage car door was open
and the flower-piled casket could be seen. A uniformed
trainman stood as its foot with hands smartly at his sides.
The blue-uniformed conductor, grasping a shiny handrail,
looked straight up at the semaphore signal to note its
position.

Within a week we were ready to say goodbye to Hemlock. My father had gone on ahead to scout the new layout
and to rent a house. He went by train, changing at Zanesville and Trinway. He also could have gone via Corning
and Columbus. One could go most anywhere by train then.
When he got back I had but one question for him: "Did you
see the Western Union office?"

There followed a farewell party and the gift of a McKinley
rocker. Pierce then ordered a box car spotted, and into this
our household goods and effects was loaded. This car in-
trigued me: I had rather expected that it would be a New
York Central car, since the Z&W was part of that system.
However, its initials were LS&MS, for Lake Shore and
Michigan Southern. Later on, I came to understand that
Pierce had acted within the Interstate Commerce rule that a
foreign car might be loaded in the direction of home.

Our new home was on a paved street. It had electric lights which cast a yellow glow, brighter but otherwise not unlike that of the oil lamp. We had hot and cold running water, a bathroom, a coal furnace, and a telephone. We were "the berries." My father chided my mother for bringing along two of her oil lamps—until she discovered that he had brought his oil lantern.

We lived on South Second Street. Just around the corner on West Walnut was Stewart's Carriage shop, where they built lovely buggies, surries, and phaetons, et al. Their sun was setting.

The panhandle of the Pennsylvania ran through the center of town, and what wonderful trains they ran, both freight and passenger! They ran solid trains of refrigerator cars with ice bunkers at either end that dripped water.

This railroad was all very intriguing, but I was not to be diverted from my then primary purpose. I had learned that it was at Western Union that the budding telegrapher grew up. Here the ham became an op, and the op a brasspounder.

The second day in town I located its magical Western Union. I managed to walk by several times, casting furtive glances through its big window. A bicycle rack on the sidewalk combined with a blue and white enameled sign that read: Western Union Telegraph Company. I had seen as many as two bicycles parked here, and so I guessed that they employed two messengers. I came at night and gazed long and intently into its dimly lit interior, although a high customer's counter hid much of this. It was easier to come at night—and for a particular reason.

On several errands that I ran uptown, I had discovered that I was something of a standout here, but not in a sense that I relished. I saw no other boys my age wearing knee-pants, as I did, and none wearing suspenders. I heard words used and others pronounced in a manner that was foreign to my habit of speech. Mulling this over, I decided that one of us spoke with an "accent," and since I was a minority of one, perhaps it was I who should try to conform.

At home I made the strongest plea I could muster for a pair of long pants. I said people stared at me and grinned. I did imagine that some did this. In a store window I had seen just what I needed: ankle length, cotton, khaki colored, and with belt loops, and for a dollar and a half. My father generously came forth with the money and with it a belt of his, which I might cut down. With the new pants my height rose about three inches and my confidence a full foot.

Furthermore, the new pants served automatically to reduce the symptoms of buck fever that assailed me at the thought of venturing into Western Union to ask about a job. I had heard that one must "strike while the iron is hot" and that "there's no time like the present." I would go the next morning. I was up early. I asked my mother if I could have a clean shirt. I wet and combed my mop of brown hair. I shined my shoes, then shined them again. I put on the clean shirt and added a necktie. I looked in the mirror and took the tie off. It didn't fit my role.

Meanwhile all sorts of thoughts ran through my head. Maybe they needed a messenger boy and maybe they didn't. Maybe they would laugh at me. Maybe they would throw me out for my temerity. Maybe they would take down my name and telephone number. One thing was sure, I was going to find out the worst.

As I was ready to leave, Ma took me firmly by the sleeve. She said, "You've been frowning all morning, did you know it? You must wipe that from your face. Take your cap off when you go in. Be sure to listen more than you talk. You'll get the job sooner or later, I know it."

The place was busy. I took off my cap and stood unobtrusively aside, waiting to be spoken to. My eyes, however, were everywhere, taking in the place's marvelous appointments. I grasped a few words of morse from among its chattering instruments and forgot to be impatient.

Then a man who had to be the boss approached me. He wore a black vest, a starched white shirt, wing collar, and black bow tie. He talked as he came. "I take it you're looking for a messenger's job," he said. "I've seen you walking by. I will have an opening come Monday morning. Be here at eight o'clock with your bike and you can go to work. The pay is eighteen a month and you can make another five if you're polite to people. You can learn telegraphy here, if that's what you want to do. Run along now, we're busy."

I nodded and left. The dreaded "interview" was over. I hadn't spoken a word. For all he knew I was a mute.

The Messenger Boy

Once again I ran home some inches off the ground. Now all that stood between me and this coveted job was a bicycle, and I would have one somehow.

Again, my father stepped into the breach and that noon went with me to Fred Decker's bicycle shop on Hickory Street. On the way there I had one misgiving. The one sled that he had bought me several years earlier was a girl's sled. He did not know that there was a difference. The girl's sled was a foot high, so that as she sat on it her skirts would not sweep the ground. The boy's sled was only half that high, and he rode "bellybuster." I got little good out of the sled, but I voiced no complaint. However, he did not now suggest a girl's bicycle, but allowed me to make the choice. He made a down payment and I was trusted to pay off the balance at four dollars a month. The cost was seventeen dollars.

Before me now lay some sixty hours in which I, a most green lad from the sticks, must learn something of this city of ten thousand. I set about this task afoot. Sunday I

Two messengers in Coshocton, Ohio, in 1915

begged off from church and walked the whole day, as I had on Saturday.

Monday morning at a quarter of eight, with a measure of confidence, I parked my shiny new bike in WU's sidewalk rack. My boss approached at the same time. He was not a person of many formalities. First off he said, "You know you must buy and wear the uniform. This will cost you a very reasonable eight dollars, which sum will be deducted from your pay at two dollars a month."

He led me to a backroom closet and pointed to one of two uniforms, which he said should fit me. It did. There was no mirror and I had to wait until I faced a store window to see what I looked like. I was really "the bee's knees," or maybe it was "the cat's meow"—if, indeed those terms had yet been invented. At any rate, I thought I looked sharp and I wished Ma could see me. Furthermore, I now had not only a second pair of long pants, but a whole new suit— navy blue and of the finest wool, plus brass buttons and a smart visored cap with the Western Union insignia across the brow.

The rest of the force now reported and the day's work was under way. A small bell tapped five times, then once. At the same time, a box whirred and extended a bit of tape on which was printed five dashes and then one, a visual confirmation of the bell taps. This was the call box. About a dozen of Western Union's pricipal patrons had a key on their wall that they could twist and, as it unwound, their individual signal would thus be recorded at Western Union. A printed card on the wall identified signal with customer. Its message was that they wanted a messenger to report.

The signal that had just come in was from American Art Works. The boss asked me, "Do you know where that is?" I said, "Yes, sir." He said, "All right, you're off." In a few minutes I was back with a sheaf of "sends," as outgoing telegrams were known here.

The long telegraph table was in the center of the floor. It was divided lengthwise by a fifteen-inch-high shelf, on which were arrayed five sets of receiving instruments in a row. On either side of this table was an operator's nook, each with the same appointments. These were a sounder-resonator, a key, a bug, and a standard-size Underwood typewriter, which sat in a well. It had pica type and, like the billing machine, was without capitals. This arrangement was designed, in part, to encourage the student's practice.

In my nine months at Western Union I did much growing

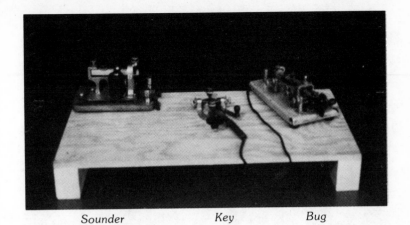

Sounder   Key   Bug

in my vocation. Here I encountered a new dimension in this field—speed. Here, the tools of speed were provided and given practice. These were the typewriter, known as the "mill" in this business, and the "bug," a patented sending device, much faster than the key and much less tiring to the wrist in the course of a protracted stint of sending. In this regard, the name Martin Vibroplex* will ring a bell in the minds of some old-timers still around. The double-speed key, also known as the "sidewinder," attained less favor.

It is probable that most beginners assumed that when they had mastered the alphabet, plus the ten numerals, they had become telegraphers. But later on they would learn that this was only first-grade staff. Before they became finished products, they would learn to use, and the use of, all the common punctuation marks, plus most of the signs and symbols found on the typewriter keyboard.

In addition to these, there would be many, many abbrevi-

---

*This was the maker's name for the "bug," a sending device much faster than the key.

The telegraph table with operator's nook and Underwood typewriter

ations for common words and phrases, all designed to promote speed. In essence, these were an extremely simplified spelling, not too hard to relate and follow. Many had trickled down into common usage from *The Phillips Code*, a dictionary of short-form language studied and practiced by press (newspaper) operators: "gg" was "going," "tt" was "that," "tts" was "that is," "cq" was "correct," "cqt" was "correct time," "ot" was "on time," "12m" was "noon," "12mn" was how we denoted midnight. I am still irked by those who write "12 A.M.," or "12 P.M.," often with meaning unclear, since there are no such hours in the day.

The Coshocton office call was CS. Messages from here were relayed through D Columbus, H Cleveland, or G Pittsburgh. In addition, CS served as the relay station for offices along the Walhonding and Wheeling & Lake Erie railroad lines. We students, when on station, kept an ear cocked for calls from either of these "jerky" lines, whence the sending would be by hand, i.e. by the slower key, and hence ideal for gaining practical experience. The first time I was permitted to answer one of these, the boss, Mr. Nathan Foresman, stood behind me and watched over my shoulder. It was a matter of pride with me that he did this only once.

He once asked me, "Where have you been learning to telegraph?" I said, "Hemlock." "Hemlock?" he said. "Do you mean Hemlock down in Perry County?" "Yes sir," I said. "Do you know where New Straitsville is?" he asked. "Yes, sir," I told him. "From Hemlock it's three miles to Shawnee, where you turn left; then it's five more miles to New Straitsville." "That," he said, "is where I was born and lived until I was about your age." We shook hands, and thereafter he was less brusque.

I was young of years, avid of purpose, and absorbent of mind, and it seemed no day went by without its lesson. There were also some never-to-be-forgotten highlights, one of which had, and still has, an eerie aspect, which I have never been able to forget.

It was County Fair week and the city swarmed with visitors. Its hotels were full. During this period, Western Union stayed open until nine P.M., and the after-hours services of one messenger were required. One evening when it was my turn at this stint, I was given a telegram bearing the address "try hotels." Nothing unusual about this, especially at fair time. The Barnes Hotel on South Fifth was nearest, so I would stop there first.

It was a balmy early October evening and a dozen or so guests occupied a row of sidewalk chairs out front. I stopped my bike at the curb and leaned forward to expose the envelope to the light from within in order to confirm the name thereon before paging this group. At that moment a tall man, wearing a large white hat and accompanied by a girl of about twelve, walked by a few feet in front of me, momentarily cutting off my light.

A step beyond, the girl stopped and said, "Papa, that boy has a telegram for you." The man looked at me and I said, "What is your name, sir?" and he gave the name on the telegram. This girl, while walking by, had read the typed name through the window envelope—in shadow and presented to her in the upside-down position. I gave her an incredulous look and she smiled sweetly at me. Her eyes looked like any other eyes, except they were prettier than most. Now, owls can swoop down from a limb in darkness and snatch a mouse from the ground. Owls, yes, but girls, no. So which was this?

It was also during this period that I made my movie debut. It was only what is called a walk-on part, although I wasn't walking. That fall, for the first time ever, a moving-picture reel was made of the whole grand spectacle of the County Fair—without sound, of course. There were views from the fairground, which included both laps of a mile-long harness race. Many mouths were open here, and you took it for granted that they were hollering. There were many shots of the bustling downtown area. There were groups here, however, that did not bustle or move much. These were would-be saloon patrons who overflowed onto the sidewalk. But largely it was a tangle of buggies, surreys, delivery wagons, and drays, plus tethered animals at hitching posts and rails everywhere, including a rail that ran the full length of Court Square on the Third Street side. There was just a sprinkling of autos, and these faced heavy going as they tried to navigate through the center of town. The horse was still in the driver's seat, so to speak.

A long panhandle passenger train from the west was pictured as it glided into the station, impressively and with authority. After disgorging another flock of fair patrons, it moved sedately out again, exhibiting great power as it gathered speed. It was doubtless pulled by the Pennsylvania's K-2 locomotive, a forerunner of the later famous K-4.

An announcement in the paper said that the Pastime Theater would show this picture, matinee and evening, on three successive days. This would be something interesting and novel to see, said I, so I attended the first evening showing. A lot of other people had the same notion, and the place was packed.

Threading the already-described scene were bicycles and more bicycles. One of these riders passed the unseen camera quite close enough to be recognized. He crossed Main Street at Hickory, rode up an alley ramp to the sidewalk and turned sharp left, now riding the left pedal. He then dropped to the walk and allowed his bike to run into the rack on its own momentum—all very efficient and business-like. This rider was I. Not suspecting that I was on camera, I gave quite a creditable performance. I went to see the picture again the second night, taking my parents. This was in 1915, however, and thus far I haven't received any offers for a screen test.

I Change Course

On the morning of November 25, I answered a call-box summons to the public library. There I was handed a telegram of birthday wishes addressed to the noted and esteemed steel magnate and philanthropist, Andrew Carnegie, who had donated the library to the city. Back at the office I asked the operator on duty if I might send this wire. He said sure and offered me his seat. Thereafter, I was to tell everybody I knew, and some others that I didn't know so well, that I had sent Andrew Carnegie a telegram.

The operator mentioned here was Frank Baird, one of the "naturals" I came to know and to follow. His interest in me and his watchfulness over my work are fondly remembered. His physique was frail, and the Spanish Flu epidemic of the 1917-18 winter claimed his life.

Perhaps his kindest gesture of all was to introduce me to his cousin, Roy Sherman, third-trick operator at Panhandle's WV tower at the east edge of town, after I had confided in Frank that I was thinking of chucking Western Union for the railroad. Roy, on his part, had suggested that I come visit him at work.

It was about midsummer of that year that a troublesome thought assailed me. Here it was July, and for the first time in memory my face, neck, and arms were a pasty white when they should have been a lusty brown. This I didn't care for. Raspberries had come and gone and blackberries were on the way out, and I hadn't set foot in the woods. It had dawned on me that Western Union's good-paying jobs would be found only in cities. And who wants to.work and live in a city! But an operator's job on a jerky railroad that ran through farm country and served farm people—ah! That would be something quite else. Further, such a job would pay at least as much, and I was to encounter more reasons corroborating my decision to alter course.

That summer somebody had brought in a thirty-five-pound sulfur-bottom catfish and displayed it for a few days in the fountain pool of Courthouse Square. It had to be seen to be believed. It was so big that, to fry, it would have to be sliced crosswise like a steak or chops. It had been caught in the Walhonding River. During Fair Week, that October, a twelve-foot cornstalk from the same area was fastened to a corner of the Gray Hardware Building at Third and Main. It had ears like bowling pins.

Farmer's produce market was a regular Saturday feature along North Third Street. Here, spring wagons in a long array were backed to the curb, and from these were offered everything the bountiful farm and woodlands provided, from the horseradish, sassafras bark, parsley, and rhubarb of spring to the apple butter, sorghum, cabbage, and nuts of fall—plus, of course, sweet corn, butter, eggs, poultry. Most of these wagons, I understood, came from the Walhonding Valley.

And the evidence mounted: Daily except Sunday a little three-car passenger train that traveled this valley pulled into the station about 9:30 A.M. to unload. It was called the Wally Flier. It terminated here and backed into clear up at WV, after turning, to await the hour of 3 P.M. when it would back down to the station to reload for the return run to Mansfield. It was hauled by a little two-driver E-7 engine, and grizzled Johnny Reese was the engineer.

When opportunity afforded, I liked to stand by and watch the people who came in or left. Mostly they were home-spun folks, who might wear dress-up clothes awkwardly. If you smiled at one of them, he or she would smile back. It was a popular little train and generally well patronized. On one occasion that I remember, the *Times Age* announced on its front page: "Wally to Fly Twice During Fair." In other words, there would be two sections, in and out.

Folks remarked what a lovely drive it was up that way, especially in harvest. Harvest was at hand and I decided to make my own tour—by bicycle, of course. I enlisted a friend who would go along. We would go the next Sunday morning, taking a lunch, some tire patches, and a pump, and journey as far as the village of Walhonding, some eighteen miles up river. I, at least, was not to be disappointed. In fact, I was not prepared for the bounty and beauty the place offered the eye.

There were miles of tall ripened corn in flat bottoms along the river. There were acres of pasture and other acres of already-harvested meadow, plus more acres of ripening second-crop alfalfa. We crossed the river through a long covered bridge, then passed through more miles of the same. It was Sunday and the horses as well as the cows were out on pasture. Some of these lifted heads high, or arched necks to gaze at us in mild curiosity. There were Jerseys, Guernseys, Holsteins, and Herefords. There were fat hogs by the hundreds. There were fields of potatoes, some partly dug. There were big barns and huge barns and much paint in evidence. I saw no drooping fences or sagging gates. It appeared a region where one couldn't go hungry if he wished. It was all in such contrast to the thin-soiled hill farms of native Perry County. This, I thought, is for me.

There was now no doubt in my mind as to where I wished to work, but problems confronted me here. One was how to proceed, and the other was my age. One was supposed to be eighteen to get a telegrapher's job on the railroad, but if I had to wait two years, I would surely die of boredom. Others, I knew had circumvented the problem. There must be a road. My mind turned to Roy Sherman and his bid to come visit him at work.

His hours were 11:00 P.M. to 7:00 A.M., so my visit, or visits, must be limited to Saturday nights, whence I might sleep in on Sunday. I would wait no longer than the coming Saturday night to respond to his invitation.

WV was definitely "big time," "main stem," "high iron." It stood beside the path of Panhandle's "extra fare" trains. These included the St. Louisian, the Keystone Express, the American, and later the Spirit of St. Louis. One paid more to ride one of these trains, but for each minute you arrived late at destination, the railroad refunded a dollar.

Some years later, when I was on third trick at Warsaw Jct., on the Wally, the operator at Trinway on the Panhandle rang me one night to say that he would leave his receiver off so that I might hear the eastbound American pass over his diamond crossing. The sound, lasting about three seconds, was something like a bushel of gravel being dumped on the floor. Later, he called back to tell me that between RD tower west of him and Conesville east of him, the American had made 103 mph. I believe that it was in the late 1920s that the I.C.C. called a halt to this risky flamboyance, to many people's relief.

In addition to Roy's primary concern with the main line, WV was the initial manual block and train order station for northward trains on the single-track Wally Branch, and thus I was to gather some valuable pointers here in this field.

One early lesson I was to gather here was that, on the railroad, telegraphy was only a means, albeit a vital means, to an end—the end requirement being to keep trains moving, but moving safely as well as expeditiously.

Also, I was to attain here a working knowledge of the basics of the interlocking machine, which would stand me in good stead in after years.

"Interlocking plant" or "machine" is an advisable term for this system, inasmuch as its moving parts are so interlinked as to prevent the operator from clearing a signal for a conflicting route. At the same time, a switchpoint must fit against the stock rail within a small tolerance. It was an English invention and patent, imported here in the late 1800s, along with expert installers. In my early days on the railroad, I came to know some of our people of the signal department who had assisted in this work, and who loved to imitate the Englishmen's speech.

Above the operator's row of huge levers, which operated his switches and signals, hung the framed and glass-enclosed blueprint, some four-by-ten feet in size, that

Tower operator Don Sanders hauls back the lever that sets switches in the yards to give a clear path to a fast freight barreling through toward Chicago. From Akron Beacon Journal, May 25, 1952

delineated the whole layout of the interlocking plant in
characters that could be read from the floor. This was illumi-
nated at night by a huge hanging oil lamp, having a large
round wick and a reflecting canopy. Further, all switch and
signal lights were oil burning, and the lamp man was a regular employee. WV had no electricity except for battery
power in connection with its communications.

I was surprised at the amount of work Roy performed on
his feet, between desk, interlocking machine, and open
window, where he leaned out to inspect passing trains.
Also, he did much of his telegraphing from a standing position. If four toots of the whistle sounded from the engine of
an approaching train, he grabbed a white light and hurried
down to trackside to watch for a note the engineer might
throw off, likely tied about a chunk of coal or an unlighted
fusee. Likewise, if the conductor in approaching displayed
a white light, held steady, it meant the same thing. These
were a couple of my initial lessons.

Roy told me that it paid to observe carefully all passing
trains and that this was a requirement of the rules. Later, I
would learn the soundness of this advice. For thus it was
that on many occasions it would be the operator on duty
who detected a hot box, sticking brakes, sliding wheels, flat
wheels, open doors of loaded box or reefer cars, a shifted
load on open-top cars, dragging equipment and, last of all,
did the train display markers at the rear.

Roy talked as he worked and would explain what he was
about. This I might understand, or might not. Mainly, I was
absorbed and quiet. I hesitated about distracting him.

He asked me how old I was. I said, "Sixteen last month."
He said "Hmmm, how long have you been telegraphing?"

I said I had started three years ago. Again he said, "Hmmm." He had one more question: "Frank tells me you're thinking of going on the railroad, is that right?" I said, "Yes, that's right. I've made up my mind, but I should tell you that I have formed an attachment for the Marietta Division, more particularly the Wally Branch," and I recited some of my reasons for this. To my relief he was sympathetic with my ambition and said he wouldn't mind transferring there himself, were it not that he would have to sacrifice his nine years of seniority. When I left, in the "wee sma" hours, he said, "Now you come back, and in the meantime I will give some thought to your problem." That was exactly what I wanted to hear him say. I felt happy as I walked home.

A week later, when I again reported at WV, Roy presented me with a current *Pennsylvania Railroad-Systems Book of Rules* and an outdated but useful Panhandle Division employee's timetable. In the rules book he pointed out two chapters at the beginning: One was titled "General Rules" and the other "General Definitions." Here, he said, was the place to start. These were basic rules, and a working knowledge of them would answer many future questions for me. Further, he told me, the rules examination, which I would some day take, would be based largely on these. Rule one in "General Definitions" described, and still describes, a train as "an engine, or more than one engine coupled, with or without cars, displaying markers."

Roy was also ready with some useful advice. He said there had never been a more opportune time to apply for a railroad job in any capacity. Business had never been better, and he predicted that should we become involved

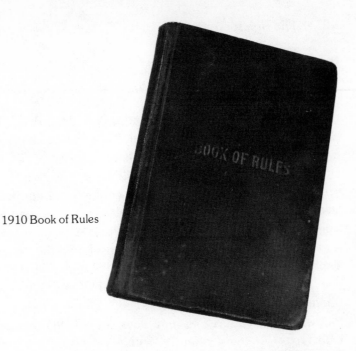

1910 Book of Rules

directly in the war in Europe, it would be all the heavier. "The railroads," he said, "sense that we will, and they are on a hiring spree. You should not overlook the fact that you may be in a position to help out. I would not advise you, however, to say that you are more than seventeen," he added. "You will by no means be the first to do this."

His further advice was that some morning when the early rush was over at Western Union I should ask for fifteen minutes off to run an errand. "Come to WV and call MN on 16 wire." MN was the personal call of George Minto, Marietta Division's Division Operator at Cambridge. "Tell him you're seventeen if you wish, and ask him if he has a job that will fit you, and leave the rest to him. In approaching him in this manner, rather than by phone or letter, you will be putting your best foot forward. He will know you can telegraph before you've said three words. You may be surprised."

I waited only until Monday morning to act. At WV I used number 16, the message wire, and called "MN, WV." The answer, "I, MN" came so suddenly I was taken aback and asked the inane question: "Mr. Minto?" He said, "es, ga" (Yes, go ahead). I gave him my brief history and said I was seventeen, feeling thankful that he couldn't see my face. I asked if he had a job that would suit me and named Roy Sherman as a reference. He said, "i, i, i," which meant he understood the question and was considering the answer. Then he told me that he would have a job that would fit my age about the middle of December. He said it was the operator-clerk job at HG. He asked, "Do you know where that is?" "Oh, yes," I told him. "I've traded WU messages with Opr. QN there often." "That," he said, "is Charley Greer. He will be a good man to post you on the block rules. It pays $35.00 a month. Give me your address and I will write you at home in a week or two."

HG was Walhonding on the Fairyland Branch—Hooray! Thirty-five dollars a month—whoopee! I would gladly wait a month or a year for such a prospect. My joy was boundless. Back at Western Union I had a hard time maintaining a straight face.

On the Railroad

Ten long days passed and I was commencing to stew when, one noon, a long envelope postmarked Cambridge awaited me at home. The first object I pulled therefrom was a round-trip pass on the Pennsylvania R.R., Coshocton to Walhonding. The rest of the news, therefore, could only be good.

Another document enclosed was a "minor's release," which one parent could sign. I asked my mother to sign it before I filled in any of the detail, which was a sneaky thing to do inasmuch as she didn't know that I would set down my age as seventeen. A hand-written note from Mr. Minto said that the official job application form would be sent R.R. mail to Walhonding, where Charley Greer would help in filling it out. Lastly, the note said I was to report on this job Monday morning, December 20, 1915. This would be my official hiring date and a matter of record to be referred to many years afterward. The note asked me to reply, and I mailed my reply on the way back to work that noon. Arriving at work, I gave Mr. Foresman nine days notice of my leaving his employ.

Since the Wally Flier didn't run on Sunday, I would have to leave home on Saturday afternoon, the eighteenth. I had told QN at Walhonding that I was to be his new helper and when I would arrive. He volunteered to speak for a "roosting and feeding" place for me, as he put it. Charley was like that.

On the eighteenth, I boarded the Wally with a heavy suitcase and a heart that matched. For the first time in my life I would live away from home and pay for my room and board. My mother had forced on me ten two-cent stamps, which in that Year of Our Lord would mail ten letters home. I told myself that I would send her the money for a new outfit for Easter. That first week away, instead of writing, I telephoned, and it was a shock to me that I didn't recognize my mother's voice. I had never talked to her on the telephone before.

When my suitcase and I touched down at Walhonding I recognized Mr. Charley Greer as the man on the baggage truck, working the BME (baggage-mail-express) car. He recognized me and spared me a grin that was better than any welcoming speech. The train gone, he took a moment to shake hands and make excuse for a week's stubble on his face. Then he hurried inside to report No. 909's arrival and departure. I then helped him move the heavy truck along the cinder platform, on which was an inch of snow. Inside, he asked me to overlook the untidiness of his floors, saying his recent helper had left the day before and that the tidying up would have to wait until next day.

From a rear window, then, he pointed out the large rambling home of Mr. and Mrs. C. B. Ogle on a nearby hillside. Mr. Ogle farmed and Mrs. Ogle kept roomers and boarders.

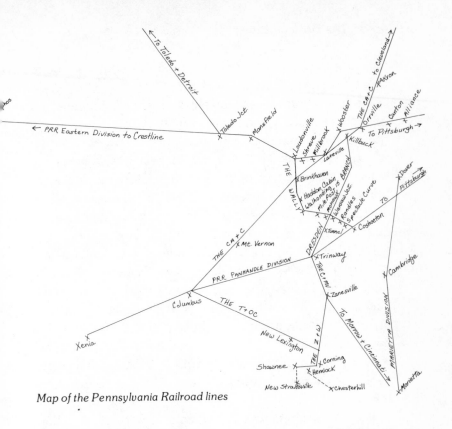

Map of the Pennsylvania Railroad lines

He said he had made reservation for me there and that Mrs. Ogle was expecting me. He said, "I'm sure you will like the place, and Mrs. Ogle's meals as well." I said, "If you say so, I'm sure I will, too."

As I climbed a path leading to a side porch, I noted the withered remains of a large vegetable garden, and through a window of a nearby chicken house I spied some lovely Buff Plymouth Rock hens. These were the best of signs, I thought, and so remindful of Hemlock. As I stepped onto the porch, a door was opened by a graying lady with twinkling eyes. She said, "Come right in." Fortunately, beside the door sat a pair of overshoes, and this reminded me to take off my own.

Inside, we introduced ourselves. She said, I understand you come from Coshocton, where people have warm houses. I'm afraid you won't find our house very warm in winter. We do the best we can to heat it with two large stoves." I assured her that this sounded very much like the home I had left just nine months earlier. She asked where that was, and I told her it was down in hilly Perry County, and that my people had been miners.

I told her I would like to pay for a week's accommodation in advance, if she would tell me how much this was. She said, "Well, I usually ask four dollars a week, or four and a half if I do the washin'. Can you afford that much?" I assured her that I could. It might be pointed out that in that day women "did the washin'," not the laundry. Too, there were washerwomen about, but no laundry women that I heard of. These were terms of the straight-razor and button-shoe age.

The upstairs here was indeed cold. The family sat about the big living room heater until bedtime. The daytime view from my window made the place seem even colder, affording as it did sight of the chilly green Walhonding River, with ice-encrusted edges, seen across bare fields.

The only concession to the Christmas season was a Juniper bough with a red bow on the table.

Early next morning, when I saw black smoke rising from the depot's chimney, I donned mackinaw coat and gloves and hustled down. Charley was at his desk. He said he wasn't expecting me till next day. I said I wanted something to do. Too, I had much to learn here and I wanted to get started, even in the smallest way. I had entered through the waiting room and noted that the big stove was plugged with ashes and clinker. I said I would clean it out. This done, I found a smashed egg crate outdoors. I used this to lay a fire ready for lighting next morning, and I brought in coal.

The wood floors here appeared to have been treated with something. The effect was much nicer than naked boards. I asked Charley about it and he said, "I'll show you my secret." In the freight house was a steel barrel of sawdust treated with oil. Before sweeping, he would sprinkle some of this about. It kept down the dust and in the course of time it had given the floors their nice finish. I had learned something and now proceeded to put it to practice.

Breaking In

Once again, as in my younger days at Hemlock, I was wrestling freight, pushing a broom, and toting the mail. Within the week I tackled minor clerical tasks, such as expense bills for incoming collect shipments. When I demonstrated that I could look up rates and compute charges on telegrams, Charley made me his Western Union manager.

The telegraph table was an interesting place where I listened avidly to train orders being sent by the train dispatcher at Cambridge and repeated by the block operators all along Marietta Division's 148 miles of track. The Marietta Division had two parts. Its main stem ran from Dover to Marietta and served the soft coal fields of Guernsey, Noble, and Washington counties. This part was 103 miles long. Its other part was the Walhonding Branch, which connected Pennsy's Panhandle Division (Pittsburgh-Columbus) at Coshocton with its Eastern Division (Pittsburgh-Crestline) at Loudonville. The Branch was 45 miles long. Coal was our "bread and butter." Much of this was termed "lake coal," inasmuch as most of it went to docks on Lake Erie, there to be transshipped by boat to ports in Michigan and Ontario. However, when the lake was ice locked in winter, the Wally Branch went to town. All our lake coal must then move overland via Mansfield, Toledo, and Detroit to reach these markets.

The Wally Branch was single track and manual block—a mode of operation whose basic purpose was simple enough: to forestall collisions. In practice it was a two-fold operation consisting of train orders (the province of the train dispatcher) and the manual block signal (the province of the block operator). In theory, trains could operate over the division in safety by either method alone, but both must be pursued. They complemented one another, but neither must lean on the other, and this point was drilled home at each periodic rules examination.

Train orders were telegraphed by the train dispatcher to the block operator and were delivered to the train by the latter. The orders were handed up from the ground clipped to a long-handled wooden hoop, which the engineer or fireman or brakie could hook with his arm as he passed. With Charley's help I learned the purpose of the green "19" and the yellow "31" train order forms, their double-faced carbons, their onionskin paper, and their writing instrument, which was the stylus.

Three forms of clearance cards were the A, the C, and the D. The form D was the nasty one. If you couldn't raise the operator at the station ahead to arrange a block indication, you stopped the train going that way, then allowed it to proceed on authority of the form D. The sleeping operator might then be due for discipline. One used the form D sparingly.

On the wall at HG, and elsewhere as well, was the switchboard, also known as the test panel, through which our wires passed coming in and going out again. Once when I heard the wire chief tell an operator to "cut out his table," I turned to Charley in puzzlement and asked, "Now what in Sam Patch does he mean by that?" Charley laughed and told me that that was what he did each night on closing up. He said it merely meant cutting or shorting out the table instruments. "I do it principally," he said, "to save on local battery."

He went to the switchboard and demonstrated how, by inserting a tapered brass plug in a certain hole, an incoming wire was jumped over to its outgoing mate, thus detouring the electrical impulse before it reached the telegraph table. He said it was a simple law of nature that an electrical current will find and follow the shortest route to wherever it is going. "It always works," he said. "It is not like man-made laws that seldom stick for long."

I had been given a basic lesson in circuitry and another in philosophy that I would always remember. In other sessions at the switchboard he cleared up the mysteries of grounding, opening, and patching, and I was greatly in his debt.

Charley, as had Roy Sherman, dwelt on the importance of markers (lights or flags), which denoted the end of any and all trains. He pointed out the engine that might have to cut away from its train and run miles for water, do a job of pushing, or double a hill (pull a train of cars up in two segments). Such engine might then, with full authority, return to its train on strength of the fact that it had displayed no markers while going the other way. It was a cardinal sin for the operator to allow anything to occupy the main between the portions of a parted train. Last, but not least, Charley said, the operator never knew when a "spotter" riding a train might take down its markers to test the operator's alertness.

Here, in short, I was wading into the intricacies of manual block railroading which would govern my steps, especially for the next ten years.

The second week in January, the pay car came along. It had left Pittsburgh several days earlier, paying along the way to Eastern Division's end at Crestline. It ran passenger extra, following the morning No. 908. It had barred windows and was hauled by a little D-16 engine. I was apprehensive as to whether it had anything for me or, indeed, that the paymaster would ever have heard of me.

It was a matter of no assurance to have to climb aboard between two guards, who looked like fugitives from a chain gang. They had eyes like jade buttons, and with as much expression. Two guns prominently displayed in belts needed only wheels to be classified as artillery pieces. The paymaster's sleeves were rolled to the elbow. He handled money like a magician did a deck of cards. When I gave my name he shoved $17.50 across the chest-high polished counter so quickly that I blinked.

I didn't count it until I was off the train. I told Charley how much I had drawn and that I had been overpaid for just eleven days' work. I asked him if I shouldn't notify Mr. Minto about this and he advised "no," observing that I had been paid exactly half a month's salary. "Some time when you see him, remember to thank him," he said.

That, I believe, was the last year for the pay car on our railroad. Thereafter, checks on a Philadelphia bank were issued and distributed by the several station agents along the line. One of these, M. L. Hauger, the agent at Mohawk, was unhappy with the new system right from the start. In addition to the added responsibility his own first check had been made out to M. L. Mohawk, Hauger, Ohio.

It was on the Walhonding Branch that I made first acquaintance with the railroad's unsung heroes. It was a warm relationship that would continue. Officially, they were called trackmen, but they went by different titles in different localities—such as section hand, paddy, gandy dancer, or pick-and-shovel artist. They were the low men on the totem pole, if you went by pay scales. But their contribution to safe railroading and their pride in a job well done were equal to that of any other craft. They worked outdoors and nowhere else, amid the steel rails that magnified the summer sun's heat and that caught and held the winters' chill.

They softened their own hard lot with a native wit and humor that featured the preposterous lie and the outrageous boast. Burl Thatcher owned probably the best watch on the division. It had 87 jewels, with holes punched for more. When asked what make it was, he proudly told you, "She's a genuine Ingersoll, and you can't buy one of 'em anywheres fer less'n a dollar."

The trackmen's yarns were often seasonal in flavor. One once announced that his wife had canned a dozen green beans the day before. "I reckon you mean a dozen cans," another said. "Yes," said the first, "a dozen cans or a dozen beans. One bean, you see, fills a can."

Another had raised a "punkin" that wouldn't go through his cellar door, so he had chopped a doorway in it and was using it for a doghouse. "It's warm and they like it," he said.

The tamping pick used on stone

The spike maul

The rail chisel

"They?" he was asked. "How many dogs have you got?"
Three," he replied. "Two hounds and a bird dog."

Their offhand remarks were often as good as their stories.
Two trackmen were assigned the task of spiking a replacement rail in place. With spike mauls they would strike alternate blows (less trying on the wind that way). One tried to beg off, saying, "You know I can't hit twice in one place." The other replied, "You're better'n me. I can't hit twice in two places."

Re the the trial of an unsavory character in County Court, one trackman remarked, "He's slippery as elm bark." Another added, "Yeah, like tryin' t' corner a rat in the roundhouse."

Another of these ever-needy souls, the head of a large family, was asked what size shoes he wore. He answered frankly, "Tens with socks, or twelves with rags."

The supply train that visited us monthly was a traveling hardware store and oil dispensary. It had three boxcars and a caboose. In one car was every conceivable tool and accessory of the trackman and car repairman. Also to be had were coal buckets, water cans, brooms, boxes of powdered glue, cans of brass polish, cakes of Bon Ami, lanterns, globes, flags, and the components of the local or wet battery. Tools were die marked with PRR insignia, and a used one was supposed to be turned in for a new one, but the rule was loosely applied. The other two cars hauled barrels of oil: coal oil, lard oil, and black oil. All this was to change in years to come, when a division engineer was to tell a supervisor of track that he couldn't supply him a pick handle without authority from Philadelphia.

Not heretofore mentioned were bales of waste, like hay

bales. Waste, true to its name, was the floor sweepings of the clothing industry. It must contain no cloth, however, only thread. Primarily the car repairman used this, doused liberally with black oil, to pack journal boxes, but everybody on the railroad found use for waste—as towels, handkerchiefs, lantern wipers, fire starters, cushions, pillows, and sometimes as a bed for the office cat.

On one occasion, I was to witness waste put to an unheard-of use.

The Rules Exam

One morning in April a well-dressed stranger got off No. 908. He was about five feet six. His shoes were shiny. He carried a light topcoat and wore a snappy black hat. He didn't belong here.

The stranger stood by with a half smile and watched as Charley and I worked the train. Then he and Charley shook hands, and I was introduced to Mr. G. A. Minto. He asked Charley when he expected the southbound local and Charley told him, "In about two hours." Then, turning to me, Mr. Minto said, "How do you feel about taking the rules examination this morning?" "The rules!" I said. My jaw dropped. The *Book of Rules* was the "operating" employee's bible. Under Charley's tutelage, I had been studying it diligently. Nevertheless, I felt unprepared to take the exam in this way, without notice. I told Mr. Minto I had thought I would have to go to Cambridge for the exam. "Ordinarily you would," he said, "but we're taking many short cuts these days as we hunt and try to enlist men."

Charley said he would run the mail uptown so we could get started. He motioned me aside and said, "Take your time and be sure you understand the questions before you try to answer." Then he added, "I'll be right back." These were four most kind words. He sensed, rightly, that I would like to feel his presence.

Mr. Minto and I retired to the now empty waiting room. His manner was easy. He prefaced many questions with "How do you understand . . ." or "How would you do . . ." this or that, and this encouraged considered answers. He would have been a good psychologist.

One direct question was: "What is the number of the current timetable?" By purest chance, I answered this correctly. The Marietta Division timetable of that time was unique. Instead of being a booklet, it was one large sheet, about thirty inches square. For office use it was tacked on the wall.

The dreaded examination was completed in about two hours instead of the anticipated eight. At its conclusion, Mr. Minto asked me to bring him a wad of waste. I supposed he wanted to dust his shoes. When I brought it, he asked me to pull out a red thread, then a yellow, a blue, a green. Then he said, "I guess you know colors. I wanted to satisfy myself on that point before we went further. When I get home," he told me, "I will send you an order to present to the medical examiner for your physical examination, but I will let you know when you are to go for it." The local whistled in and he went out to board the caboose.

I was elated, but Charley's face was sober. He said, "It won't be long now." I said, "What won't be long now?" "Until you are shipped out," he told me. "I have come to know the signs. You are number four that I have broken in." I felt sorry for him. His was a burdensome job. We had been friends.

On My Own

May had arrived, and my only word from Cambridge had been a switch key in the mail. It bore a serial number, and with it was a receipt which I would sign and return. This key remains one of my mementos.

It was closing-up time one evening, but we both seemed reluctant to leave. There would be something more to do, was the feeling. We sat around and made small talk. Charley remarked, "The whiteoak leaves will soon be as big as squirrels' ears." "Yes?" I asked. "That's when the farmers about will start planting corn," he said. Then only the clock was heard. It was like the stillness that follows when a flock of chattering sparrows suddenly takes off.

Then No. 16 wire clicked open. It was the one with the tobacco tin attached to its sounder to give it a distinguishable voice. Then came, "HG, MN." I looked at Charley and he said, "You answer." I did so and Mr. Minto asked, "GS?" I said "esr" (yes, sir). He said, "You open up RA tomorrow nite at 10K (ten o'clock). All supplies will be inside. The door and the oil box will have switch locks on them.

That will be your job until further notice." I said I would be there.

RA Randles, a cabin job, was but five miles up the valley from home. But for some reason I didn't smile at this word. My reaction was more like shock. Even by the railroad records I would not be eighteen until that October—really seventeen. It was as though I, having added a year to my age, my boss, wishing to be equally generous, would now add another five months.

With genuine regret I took leave of the Ogles and of Charley the next morning. In the past five months he had guided me far along the road of my ambition. Often afterward when a problem arose, I would think back and ask myself what Charley had said about it, and I would have the answer.

Riding home on No. 908, my emotions ran wild. Maybe, after all, I should have stayed with Western Union where I would not hold people's lives in my hands every day. But I knew I would not turn back. One should not shirk either work or responsibility, so I had heard. I could now claim the title of brasspounder. I would make a whopping fifty-five dollars a month. My folks, I knew, would be proud of me. I would live at home again.

When No. 908 passed RA, I was out on the back platform to give the place the once-over. At the top of the signal mast were the two movable semaphore blades, now in the upright position where they should be until 10K that night, when I would drop them to the horizontal position, indicating the office was open. I noticed the steel oil box and also the two iron castings on the building's front, from which I would display train order signals. There was a small pile of coal across the tracks. The place looked as though it expected me.

Back home, I greeted Ma and Pa warmly after five long months. My old yellow bike patiently awaited me in the out-kitchen. I pumped up its tires. It, too, would now go to work for the railroad. Uptown I bought the first of several lunch boxes that I was to own. "Dinner buckets" we called them down in Perry County, and I was a long time in learning to call them by another name.

Ma busied herself fixing a homecoming supper. There was jelly and a pie made from about the last of her Perry County blackberries. There were hot soda buscuits on which one piled much butter and jelly. She urged me to take a nap after supper, but sleep had never been farther from my thoughts.

I left home at eight and let myself indoors at RA before nine. I lit a lamp, which somebody had thoughtfully filled with oil. I cut in my wires at the test panel and was gratified to hear each click closed. I then satisfied myself that all stationery supplies were on hand. Among these was a railroad-issue iron-pointed stylus for writing train orders. Train order paper was unique stuff—thin, slick, and rather durable. If the double carbons were in good condition, one could make eight or ten readable copies by bearing down on the stylus. The railroad styluses' iron points were never too smooth, in spite of frequent polishing on the soft leather uppers of one's shoes. Before long, I answered a newspaper ad and acquired an agate stylus of my own, which served me well for many years thereafter.

On the floor were two bullseye lamps for the signal mast (with their prism lenses which magnified and directed their beam), and four new lanterns. In each of the latter were new wicks, woven of coarse cotton thread. Now, one had to know his stuff in order to trim a new one in exact symmetry. You proceeded by dipping the tip lightly in coal oil, then lighting it and allowing it to burn dry and char down to the metal sleeve. Then you brushed it off with your finger, creating a perfect horizontal. When you raised and lit it, it would burn in a symmetrical half moon. You had to be from Perry County to know about this. The fuel for these lanterns was lard oil, and in real cold weather the lard oil can had to be kept indoors else it wouldn't pour. The lamps for the signal mast burned signal oil, which was another name for coal oil.

Promptly at 10K I checked in with DS, the dispatcher at Cambridge, with WV at Coshocton to the east of me, and with WJ at Warsaw Junction to the west. Then I dropped my fixed signals to stop and RA was officially open for business. I blocked a half-dozen freights by my station, with no meets and no orders to hand on. Not until the eastern sky grew pink did drowsiness assail me.

At RA, I had a few lessons to learn the hard way. Once my father gave me a large green desk blotter which he thought I might like to have on my telegraph table. I thought so, too. I came to work early and brought the blotter, together with an idea. Instead of trying to fit it around my three sets of instruments, I would lift these, then return them to place on top of the blotter. The result was a neat and professional-looking job, and I was pleased with myself.

Several nights later, I reported only a few minutes early and cut in my wires. The dispatcher's line was busy—nor-

The trainman's lantern

mal enough—but, to my consternation, his morse was coming in on all three lines, including the block wire, which didn't go to Cambridge.

A look at my desk told me why. A large section of my nice blotter had turned a dark green. It was watersoaked from rain that had beaten in at a window. I opened my dispatcher's key, thinking to report my difficulty, but nothing happened. This, too, was shorted out. I quickly cut out again and went feverishly to work undoing all my nice handiwork. Finally, twenty minutes late, I checked in. I explained my tardiness by saying I had found water on the table, but about the blotter I was discreetly mum. I took steps to see that it didn't happen again, however. Next

The trackwalker's lantern

night I brought along a pound of putty—you bought this in bulk then, as you did a pound of lard—and the loose window was tightly sealed from top to bottom.

At RA, I found that I didn't know as much about colors as I thought I did, nor as much as Mr. Minto had credited me with knowing. I thought it might be provident to supply myself with an extra globe for each of my lanterns, so I filled out what was called a "material transfer" order, requesting one globe each of white, red, yellow, and green. When the carton arrived, I opened it in daylight to check on my order. The red, the white, and the yellow were fine, but the green globe requested was anything but green. It was a lovely sky blue.

Ha! Somebody was testing me, I thought, and I packaged this globe for return, along with a pointed note. However, I had learned that one should think twice before acting once. I would make a test. At work, I lit my green lantern, then exchanged its globe for the new one. The light it gave was just as green with one as with the other. When daylight came and both were held to the sky, one was just as blue as the other. It was the yellowish flame within that wrought the magic change in color.

I kept the globe and destroyed my note.

Long Nights, Bright Days

Today, many jobs are of the monotonous assembly-line variety. But on the railroad, as I look back, it seems no two days were ever the same. I was not appreciative of this. The proper attitude one took to work was "Expect anything, and eventually it will happen." There would be days and nights when time dragged and others when one could have used an extra pair of hands.

Silence has been called golden, but it seems to have gone out of style today. Many panic in its presence. If it threatens, they must at once seek or create noise. But it is in silence that truth is perceived, reason is born, and perspective developed.

Reading matter was banned in the block station, but the rule against smoking didn't apply there, so on the way to work one night I stopped in a poolroom and bought a can of tobacco and a genuine "Missouri Meerschaum" pipe. Each cost ten cents. These proved a help. They have been companions of mine ever since.

I wished I had a dog, but that would have been impractical. I did, however, acquire a couple of visitors about this time, who remained to become regular boarders. They were a pair of young mice. One I trained to climb my pants leg and eat a bit of cheese from my knee. If the cheese wasn't there, he stood on his hind legs and looked at me inquiringly. This act became a regular ritual at midnight, as though he read the clock on the wall.

There *was* a clock there, a faithful old Seth Thomas that required winding every eighth day with a provided key. Its unhurried tick-tock measured off the night in slow cadence.

October arrived, a breath of winter was in the air, and I was having a nightly fire. As I arrived at RA one night, an unaccountable uneasiness assailed me. This was most unusual. I had never felt anything like fear or dread before. I looked about me for cause, but there was no cause, nor was there any assurance. The switch lamp across the tracks burned, but its two eyes, one green and one red, stared back at me in cold indifference. A tree, now bare, made a silhouette against the night sky that suggested a skeleton, and its limbs rattled softly in the breeze. It was not hard to imagine the rustling of some leaves on others to be the whispering of conspirators. A puff of air from no apparent source fanned my face. Had it been a bat on the wing, or a witch on a broomstick?

Indoors, I lit my lamps and started a fire. This should have eased the uneasiness, but it didn't—quite. The old clock ticked too loudly, as though it meant to betray my presence to something or somebody. I wished a train would come along. At midnight, I opened my lunch box and first-off took out the customary chunk of cheese. My friendly mice would soon appear.

But 12:05 came, and 12:10, and no mice! I thought I understood the reason. Rats were known to abandon the sinking ship and mice, I judged, could be expected to behave likewise. I could generate no cheerful thought. It now occurred to me that Halloween was just in the offing when, as all knew, ghosts and goblins, spirits and sprites were wont to take over and rule the night. My own spirits drooped some more.

It was at this moment that a great hoot owl in the nearby woods shattered the deep stillness with his eerie cry. A chill began at my lower spine and coursed upward to the collarbone. Had I been a dog, I know my hackles would have risen. From a mile off, across the river, came an echo, faint but distinct. But no! It was not an echo, but a reply! I now diagnosed these hoots and realized to my dismay that these fiends were sending morse, and right over my head! The cry of each consisted of three notes, all of the same pitch, but spaced differently. The first had sounded "0 00" which was the R in morse. The second had replied with "00 0" which was the C in morse. Had they succeeded in sounding RA, my office call, I would no doubt have panicked. But they had made a mistake, even as we humans do, and this proved a saving thought.

Otherwise, I might have reacted as did a band of immigrant English Quakers, of years ago—according to a legend in our family. They had halted their little caravan at the crossroads settlement of Chesterhill down in Morgan County, Ohio, where they meant to encamp for the night. But, with the fall of darkness, a hundred, or maybe a thousand birds of the night sent up their chant of "whippoorwill, whippoorwill." The good Quaker folks thought they sang

"Chesterhill, Chesterhill." Taking this to be a dire omen, they hastily rehitched and dug out of there. The legend didn't say how far they might have gone in trying to escape the omnipresent song of the whippoorwill on a summer's night in the forest.

Nights at RA were long (though few so long as that eerie eve in October). But interest and expectancy livened when the footlights came on in the east. The curtain would soon rise on another day, and for this reason I was to conclude that sunrises were nicer than sunsets.

One spring morning there was a faint aroma and the sound of many bees in the air. It was an inviting scent and I looked about for its possible source but without luck. The aroma grew noticeably on succeeding mornings until, with my door open, it flooded the interior and drowned out the smell of oil lamps. My frustration deepened as I tried vainly to locate its origin.

There was a clue that I could have followed had I been wise enough. A hundred yards away a big tree stood in a fence row. It was not a pretty tree in a symmetrical sense, but I had noticed it greening more each day as its leaves developed. On another morning, with the sun's rays full on it, there was a change. Spots and patches of pink and white could be seen. A morning or two later the whole tree was transformed. It had dressed itself up for spring in an all-new flowered gown. It was beautiful. It was center stage. It was the elusive font of the all-pervading perfume. On inquiry, I learned that it was a honey locust.

One morning, after work, I walked that way, and the air was filled with a fine hum. A million bees were carting away its nectar. On returning, I took notice of the bees that flew directly over my head. They were doing the best they could to point out to me that which I had been seeking, as they flew in a "bee line" directly to or from the big flowered tree. Well, anyhow, it would be something to remember next time.

That spring season, Sells-Floto Circus, having shown in Coshocton, moved up the branch one night, heading for Mansfield. There were two sections. These ran passenger extra and were accorded the right-of-way.

As the second section left WV's yard somebody reported to the operator an animal cage door swinging open on one of the cars. I heard the operator at WV make this report to our dispatcher and add that this was on the fireman's side. This would be on my side of the track as well, and I knew what was coming next: a message for the train's crew notifying them of the circumstance, which same I would hand on as they passed.

I was in the middle with no way out. I slowed the train and took my position beside the track with order hoops and white light. I spotted the partly open cage door when it was a car length away. I ducked quite low—not that the door would strike me, but I didn't fancy whatever might be inside striking me either. I watched as the conductor, with white light swung down on the engineer, then some forty car-lengths up the track. I gave my report to the dispatcher and he, thinking to be funny told me I had better keep my door shut for the rest of the night. I told him I had already thought of that.

In fall and winter, travel by bicycle was impractical. Thus, when opportunity afforded, I bought myself a used Fairbanks-Morse speeder. The dictionary calls these velocipedes, describing them as three-wheeled railroad handcars, and lets it go at that.

But speeders were much more than that. They were a marvelous means of getting about over the railroad in good weather or bad, and to own one was a sort of status symbol. It proclaimed the the rider was a railroader, and of some privilege, else he would not be allowed to have and operate one.

The speeder was primarily the vehicle of the car inspector and the lineman. Its two main wheels rode the right-hand rail, and the third, smaller one was an idler at the end of a reach, which rode the other rail for stability. Propulsion was by means of a pair of upright handles, which the rider rocked back and forth as he sat. At the bottom of these was a pair of stirrups he pushed with his feet. A small platform behind him was for tools. If he carried no tools, a passenger could ride there, facing backward.

When the rail was damp with dew, and by dropping the hands halfway down the handles a fella could go from one milepost to the next in three minutes, and that was a spanking 20 mph. If a train bore down on him, he could make an "emergency landing" by leaning hard right, upsetting the rig onto the sixfoot. The rigs were sturdy and could take it.

To elucidate, the sixfoot was an area of that width extending laterally from the outside rail of main tracks. The first two feet of this was white limestone, screened to three-inch size and neatly confined. Primarily, this was a ballasting material, useful for drainage, for shoring up the low joint, and thus maintaining a smooth rail surface. This was accomplished by means of the curved stone, or tamping pick—another relic of yesterday.

Advertisement for a speeder built by the Sheffield Velocipede Car Company in 1880

Advertisement for a handcar built in 1880

The other four feet was a continuous manicured strip, ever a constrasting black from the shower of fine ash that belched from the stack of the working engine. However, the chief purpose here was a safe footing for the trainman who must alight from or board a train in daylight or darkness. It also somewhat softened the landing one made if he had to upset his speeder.

Speeders were ingeniously designed things, yet one wondered sometimes what all went through the inventor's mind as he put the contraption together. If he had set out deliberately to build a machine on which the rider would get soaking wet in a shower, I don't see how he could have done better, as the driver sat and propelled it with arms and legs fully outstretched.

That was my condition when I arrived at RA at ten o'clock one night. I had matches in my pocket, yes, but they were water soaked and useless. A groping search of the pitch-dark interior was of no avail. The siding switch lamp, a few yards away, was out. I was dismayed. If I stopped a big train because I displayed no block lights, I might be charged with incompetence. I had one chance left, but it seemed a dim one. Seventy-five car lengths up the track would be a switch lamp at the other end of the siding. Since this switch was on a curve, its lamp was atop a ten-foot standard to afford greater visibility for the approaching train. At the same time, being this high off the ground, it was the more exposed to buffeting winds. I boarded my speeder and took off. When I rounded the curve, some twenty car lengths short of the switch, glory be! I could see its gleaming green eye. Ever so carefully, I brought down the lamp. Pumping the speeder with one hand, I carried the lamp gingerly in the other. From its small flame I lit all my lamps. Then I returned it to its place. The day was saved, and never again would I be caught without dry matches.

The speeder, since it required no steering, allowed one to gawk about and take in one's surroundings as one rode along. The characteristic features of a regularly traveled route soon became familiar, but out in the country these were ever changing and never dull. The activities of people and of creatures and growing things varied from season to season.

On spring mornings, with the grass and weeds heavily wet with dew, young rabbits and whole families of ground-nesting birds such as quail, pheasant, and killdeer would emerge onto the graveled sixfoot to dry out. Most retreated into the weeds at the speeder's approach. But a certain well-remembered mother quail and her little brood did not. Instead, she would set the example by crouching quite low to the ground, and her babes would all follow suit. I would drop my hands to my lap and coast by, pretending not to notice them. The little ones looked the size and softness of marshmallows, and in their motionless pose they might have been mistaken for gravel stones. This tableau was repeated at the same spot and at the same time on several successive mornings.

One morning, my speeder and I were rounding Spectacle Curve on the way home. At this point the track closely bordered a stretch of the old Ohio Canal. This section still ran bank-full of water and served to power a hydroelectric plant near Roscoe. I presume my eyes popped as I beheld, upside-down in the water, a boxcar, complete except for its trucks, which rested on the sloping bank. I felt sure it had not been there when I passed this way in the darkness of the night gone.

A door had sprung open, revealing the lading to be something in paper bags. I could also read its initial and number a foot under water. There were some scarred ties, but as far as I could tell, the track was in good line and there were no raised spikes. I recalled that a southbound freight in the night had been slow in clearing this block. This might be a clue.

Arriving in town, I went to WV for a look at his block sheet. This showed the train in question as having "gone by" this station, rather than having arrived and departed.

The fact that the train had not been stopped at WV indicated that it had lost its running time elsewhere.

I gave the particulars to the Cambridge dispatcher, and it was news in his office. The train's conductor, when contacted, said his train had parted on Spectacle Curve, but that they had recoupled promptly and proceeded. The delay not being serious, he had not considered a report of the incident necessary.

As already pointed out, on the railroad no two days or nights were alike. Another observation in this vein was: If it can happen, it will. Still, it was not reasonable to expect that a freight conductor might lose a loaded boxcar from his train and not know it. But then, it can happen . . . and so it *did*.

The Wally Flier

A half mile north of me was Randles Station. It was a little cinder platform level with the ties, and that was all. It was a flag stop for the Wally Flier. At a farm home in the vicinity lived a maiden of several summers come and gone, who taught the piano and had a clientele in the city. She rode the Wally twice a week. About half the time she made the station, and the other half Johnny Reese would have to stop his train for her somewhere beyond. In these cases, both the handsomely uniformed conductor and the brakeman would have to alight and lift her up to the first step. I thought she rather enjoyed this.

The Wally line and its little passenger train were the butt of many jokes of the Toonerville Trolley type. Some were apt and some were applied—there's a fine difference.

It was August and it was hot—hot and muggy, sticky and humid. Lethargy was epidemic, inertia was chronic. Chickens stood about with wings akimbo and the birds could find nothing to sing about. The expression "hotter'n the hinges o' hell" could be heard several times a day. Every dog you saw had his tongue hanging out three to six inches, depending on his size and the thickness of his coat.

As the story was told, the little passenger train stood at the station. Its sweltering human cargo had one concerted wish: that the train get moving again so there would be a stir of air through the few windows that could be opened.

A lady got aboard, lifted a small basket with a neat cover to the overhead rack, then sat down beside the seat's other occupant, a fat, bald, suffering man with shirt open, who slumped rather than sat. A droplet, then another, fell from the basket and landed on his head. From there they coursed down his cheek to the corner of his mouth. He stuck out his tongue to savor them. Turning only his eyes he asked, "Honey?" The lady, moving only her lips, replied, "No, puppy."

Once at County Fair time an extra coach was added to the Wally Flier. At either end of it was an innovation, double-hinged or swinging doors—an ill-conceived idea in this instance.

An elderly man with a long flowing beard was returning home with a prized purchase he had made at the fair—a gallon of luscious, thick sorghum molasses in a glass jug. He had nursed and nurtured this for much of the day and he was now almost home. Doubtless he smacked his lips at the prospect of buckwheat cakes and sorghum in the winter months ahead.

He was leaving the train, hugging the precious jug against his body with both hands, when the person ahead allowed the door to fly back, smashing the jug to smithereens and plastering the poor man's entire front, beard and all. He stood still in horror and bewilderment. A few laughed. Most

Advertisement for a coach lamp built by Post and Company in Cincinnati in 1880

commiserated. "What if it had been a woman carrying a baby?" someone ventured. One of the passengers quickly appeared with a bucket of water and a broom from the station and did his best to reassure and comfort the old man while scrubbing him down.

On a morning of late April another passenger for the Wally approached RA cabin, walking slowly up the track and carrying two half-bushel baskets, which were obviously heavy. He was small, elderly, and narrow of shoulder. He had a wide mustache that was white except for a section in the center, which was tobacco stained. He wore steel-rimmed glasses. He might have been called shabby, but his was a neat shabbiness. He was affable. On this first occasion, he stopped and asked about the train, then asked if he might come in and set his watch, which had stopped. It was twenty minutes till train time and and I asked him how he had judged this. "By the shadders," he said.

But where had he come from? He was not a local farmer taking eggs to town, else he would have driven horse and buggy. The question was answered when he lifted the cloth cover of one of the baskets to show me six catfish. They were of near-uniform size and would weigh, I thought, about five pounds apiece. Thus, his load weighed some sixty pounds for the two baskets. He was taking them to Coshocton, where a certain restaurant would buy them and pay him more than would the butcher. I said, "Where do you live?" He said, "Down by the river. You'll have to come visit my place some day." He said his name was Holly Randles.

I offered to set the speeder on and run his load up to the station. "That will be real clever of you," he said. ("Clever," in years gone by, was used to denote a kindness or accommodation, or a person who was kindly disposed.) This I did, setting the baskets on the platform, then waiting a few minutes for him to come closer before I returned to the cabin. I was to do the same on future occasions.

A Visit into Yesterday

The more I thought about Holly's invitation the more I thought this might be something interesting to do. The next time I saw him I asked if I might come the following Monday and stay the day. He said, "Of course. I'll be ready for you."

Thus, on Monday morning after work, I reported, taking along six packages of Buckshoe which I had noted was his brand of chewing tobacco. This visit is still memorable. It was a step back into another age. "Primitive" and "practical" are a couple of words that fit here.

His home was neither cabin nor tent, but a combination of the two. It was about ten feet square and boarded up to a height of about five feet. The rest was a peaked canvas top. It was a warm May morning and on my approach I was most puzzled to note icicles hanging from the edge of its south slope. I had to ask about this, and Holly explained that he had treated the canvas with melted paraffin and that the hot sun had remelted some of it and caused it to run down and form these dangles.

The site was on private farmland where it "tailed out"

79

near the river. It was grown up in trees and scrub and had a gravelly topsoil. I gathered that he was quite welcome here as a squatter, especially since several farm wives about were more than glad to trade eggs, milk, and butter for fresh-caught fish throughout the summer.

The cabin's appointments were basic: a stove, a cupboard, a bed, and a table. The bed was, more aptly, a bunk, or a bin. It was nailed to two of the walls, in a corner. It was two feet deep and filled with oats straw—softer than wheat straw. It had a duck cover or spread. A cord dangled from above and hung down near the feather pillow. The small stove was of cast iron and flat topped. It was not in use at this time, but on top was piled an armload of wood for emergency use. The cupboard was nailed to the wall, with brackets underneath. The table was hinged to the wall and had one folding leg. These furnishings were all two feet or so above the packed earth floor, this to keep them clear of floodwaters that might visit on occasion. A large iron skillet doubled as a dutch oven. A large dishpan doubled as a washtub. He had a washboard. His toiletries were a straight razor, a bone comb and a bar of yellow, home-made, all-purpose soap. He had a can of tallow for his shoes. Obviously this was no short-term fishing camp. Indeed, he had said that he lived here.

Nearby, at the river's edge, was a huge pile or more properly a windrow, of driftwood. This, I judged, had influenced his choosing the spot for a place to live. In the beginning he had salvaged a rowboat from the pile, quite usable but lacking oars. Since then it had provided the lumber that went into the building of his hut, plus numerous skinning boards on which fur pelts would be stretched for curing, come winter. Moreover, it was an endless source of firewood and backlogs, all usable with little chopping or sawing.

When I arrived that morning, he was preparing breakfast at an outdoor fire. This would be bacon, eggs, and milk toast. In a cast-iron skillet, most black on the outside, bacon was frying. Near the edge of the fire a pan of milk with a large chunk of butter afloat was warming. When the bacon was forked out, eggs were broken into the skillet. And here I was to learn about frying eggs to the soft stage. After they had fried about twenty seconds, a couple of tablespoons of water were added to the hot skillet and a lid was held on tightly for another ten seconds. Then they were done and lifted out, softly cooked, top and bottom. A slice of bread that had been toasting in a bent-wire arrangement was placed in the bottom of a pan. On this was forked a fried egg and overall was poured the hot buttered milk. After three of these servings I thought I had never had such a satisfying breakfast before. He served coffee, too, black as a witch's heart and as bitter. I drank a cup anyway.

As the place was being tidied up, he announced that he was going to the woods for the day to hunt ginseng and yellow root. The camp would be mine and he assured me that nothing would disturb my sleep. he came in presently with a green walnut branch. he pounded this with a stick to bruise its leaves. Then he tied it to the cord that hung above the bunk. This was my mosquito repellent. It was quite effective.

He told me we would have blue cats and fresh peas for supper. Then he was off. His digging tool resembled a mason's chipping hammer. The other tool was his pocketknife.

I woke in midafternoon sorely in need of a drink. I

dressed and went outdoors in quest of some water, but could find none. I thought of going to the river but told myself I'd better not drink from it. Then I heard Holly returning. He had read my thoughts and said, "I bet you're lookin' for a drink. I forgot to show you my cave this mornin'. Come with me." He led me to a dense spot in the thicket. Here two wide boards covered a four-foot-deep hole, at the bottom of which was a gallon stone jug of drinking water with a corncob stopper, plus a bucket in which were butter, eggs, and milk. A wire with a hook at the end was nearby and with this the jug or the bucket could be lifted out.

The water was cool and palatable and I asked him where he had got it. He said, "Come with me and I'll show you my well." The well was on a sandbar some forty feet from the water's edge. It was about two feet deep and half full of water, which must be ladled out carefully to avoid roiling the sand. It was open to the sky and this, plus the fact that it was filtered through many feet of sand, assured its purity, he told me. I have never had reason to doubt this.

He said, "Let's go to the garden and pick some things for supper." I hadn't guessed that he had a garden, but he had. The boat was shoved into the water and poled some fifty feet to the shore of a small island, ownership of which was claimed by no one. The soil here was pure river silt and on it he grew, in small amounts, about everything that a summer garden might be expected to yield, including tomatoes, sweet corn, and melons yet to ripen. We picked the very first yield of peas, plus crisp leaf lettuce and long white icicle radishes. An unforeseen advantage here, he told me, had been the absence, so far, of rabbits.

Holly exhibited surprising skills as a cook, and supper that evening was a pure feast. he assured me that it was easier to cook for two than for one. From a "fish box," which resembled somewhat a chicken crate, submerged in the water, he pulled out three live "blue cats," each weighing something over a pound. It must be noted here that to the fisherman it was not sufficient to call a catfish a catfish. One must be more specific. There were the huge sulfur bottoms, the shovel or bullheads, and the smaller blue or lady cats. These last were, in Holly's opinion, the sweetest of them all. Moreover, they need not be skinned before frying. Supplementing the fish for supper were creamed peas, lettuce wilted in bacon grease and diluted vinegar, and crisp radishes. That meal is still a fond memory.

The meal over and the dishes washed, it was time to relax awhile before bedtime. But not indoors. By no means indoors. It was outdoors where the beauty, the music, and the interest now lay. Holly said, "In summer it's the nicest part of the whole day." So we retired to the campfire, where we sat on a log and listened; listened and watched. As Holly put it, we would "listen to the quiet." The sounds, he said, "were all different from day sounds."

To be heard were pond frogs, tree frogs, crickets, screech owls, and "twitter birds." Sometimes a 'coon would be heard scratching in the gravelly shore for mussels. Sometimes a field mouse squeaked as it was caught in the owl's talons. A mile down river a horse and buggy might rumble across the iron bridge. Sometimes a fish jumped in the water. Sometimes, from a half mile off, might be heard the frantic drumbeat of a grouse's wings as it flew from its ground roost in terror of a marauding fox or weasel. If one looked up at the right moment, he might see a bat fly by on soundless wings. A skunk might approach within a few feet and, raising one front paw, quietly study the camp scene awhile, then walk slowly away. Looking around, one might see a dozen pairs of tiny eyes reflecting the red glow of the fire. All the while, a riffle in the nearby river supplied unobtrusive background music.

And stars! There was no end to them. The darker one's immediate surroundings the more stars one sees and the nearer they appear. The scene was frequently pierced by the grand arc of a meteorite or "shooting star." One leaves such a scene with a keen sense of one's own insignificance.

We talked softly. He told me that as a poor boy without shoes it was his job to bring in the cows for milking. When the ground was frost covered he had learned to turn over a flat rock and stand in the spot and warm his feet. Once, when the fire at home went out, he was sent across fields to a neighbor's to fetch a live coal. Flint, steel, and tinder they had, but no "strike matches." These were not common in the 1860s. As a young man he had trapped the last known otter on this stretch of river. He blamed the digging of the canal and the increased activity it brought for their disappearance.

He had worked much on farms of the vicinity, and his service as a builder of haystacks or hayricks was much in demand, I was to learn. He presently maintained two trotlines in the river, which he "run first thing of a mornin'," with the aid of his boat. A trotline was one that reached from bank to bank, as distinguished from the throwline, which was thrown into the water from the shore. He fished for catfish, which brought the best price in the market. He accomplished this, he said, by bottom fishing, in other words weighting his lines to the river bed where catfish fed. He had never worked a day indoors and seemed to be proud of it.

He would stay here, he said, until sometime in November "'pendin' on the weather," and do a little trappin' for muskrat, mink, skunk, and 'coon. "Did you ever eat a muskrat?" he asked me. "You'll have to try one sometime. They're real good."

The air was sweet and sleep inducing, and when he started scraping ashes against the glowing backlog, to keep it alive till morning, I knew he was tired and I said I must be going. He said, "Don't forget your lunch on the table, and don't forget to come back." I didn't know he had fixed a lunch for me. It was a huge catfish sandwich and several white radishes with the salt added.

Time

Back at my job that night, I was to marvel at how different was my world from Holly's. Here we lived by the clock and would be truly lost without it, and I recalled Holly's description of an early settler's "timepiece." Not all backwoods folks had clocks in those days, but still they managed a close approximation of time by means of a device. This, in essence, was a vertical crack in a south door which, at high noon the third week in June, cast a narrow beam of sunlight across the floor in the northward direction. At this time the beam's path would be scratched in the floor boards. By this a clock, if they had one, could be set at twelve noon with reasonable accuracy.

On the railroad, time was of the first essence on a twenty-four-hour-a-day basis. Time and the timetable, plus reliable communications, were prime factors on the single-track manual block system, and these went hand in hand. The inferior train must not encroach on the time of the superior train. A train might be superior by right, class, or direction. Right was conferred by train order, class, and direction by

Engineer's vest watch

time table, so the book said. Further, the engineer's "speed-ometer" was his watch, plus the mileposts along the way. Both he and the conductor must have "standard" watches. These must be of twenty-one or more jewels. They must be submitted for periodic inspection by a designated watch-maker, at least one of which was to be found in any city along the railroad. The operating employee's watch was of eighteen size and weighed four ounces, or a quarter of a pound. Most always, the engineer's watch was carried in the bib pocket of his overalls, where it afforded ready access as he sat at the throttle. It would be anchored there by a shoestring or a leather thong. The time table listed several stations where standard clocks were located, with which watches might be compared.

Block operators were not subjected to these rigid requirements, the telegraph ever affording them access to the correct time. Generally this was had by a glance at the clock when the dispatcher completed a train order. However, if he wished to reduce this to a split hair, he had recourse to the Arlington time signal, broadcast over the telegraph twice daily at 11.00 A.M. and 11:00 P.M. (I speak here of the Central Time Zone, which at that time encompassed us. Later, we would become part of the Eastern Time Zone.)

The old Seth Thomas clock was probably as trustworthy as any watch then extant, provided it was accorded a bit of intelligent care and attention. Many of these still run sixty-odd years later. If one detected a minute variance in the interval between the tick and the tock, versus the tock and the tick, the clock hung out of plumb. If it lost time, the weight at the bottom of the pendulum was screwed up a hairsbreadth, thus shortening its stroke a mite. If it gained time, you did the opposite. One station agent, more of a perfectionist than most, kept a small wad of waste lightly dampened in coal oil in the bottom of the case. The fumes arising from this, he said, kept the works lubricated. He also relied on a homemade plumb bob to keep his clock hanging just so.

Engines and Engineers

The Pennsy owned a lot of locomotives, some great, some small, some fast, some slow, and others in between. We had sixty-five pound (per yard) rail on our division, each rail thirty-one feet long, and the heaviest engine these would accommodate was the H-6.

Listening to the earnest talk of many engineers over the years, one came to understand that engines were not just machines—tools or facilities used in the course of a day's work and then forgotten. Not at all. Engines had personality, individuality. Often they were credited with human attributes that endeared them to these, their handlers. A new brakeman, sharing the fireman's seat on the other side of the cab, might sometimes show concern when he thought he heard the engineer talking to the engine.

As I have said, things were personal then. That railroads of the era were so prosperous was due in no small measure to a sense of cooperation and enthusiasm among the rank and file. They succeeded as did the beehive or the anthill, where each individual contributed his willing bit. Sophistication, automation, and the burgeoning of unrealistic rule and command were to discourage much of this.

The employee's time table was supposed to be a quick reference book for all concerned. It was of most particular concern to the engineer of the moving train. The unrealistic proliferation of command is exemplified by a comparison of Eastern Division's time table No. 7B of April 5, 1914, and one of many years later. The former, while listing the schedules of 151 passenger trains on this one panhandle division, contained just sixty-five printed pages. The latter, embodying four divisions of the railroad, listing a total of 59 passenger trains, contained 288 printed pages plus 96 blank pages in the back for posting general orders. Profit and expediency were beginning to prevail. "Safety First" was still preached, but in hollow tones.

Among the freight engines, the least in size on our division was the homely little class R. It was, however, probably the most esteemed. It was tough, ugly, determined, and dirty—and glad of it. Some said it chewed tobacco. It knew nothing and cared less about streamlining. It was happiest when at work. It had four drivers of fifty-inch diameter and nonslippery habit. Its boiler popped at 150 pounds. It was most responsive to the throttle. I have imagined that its rhythmic "chug-chug, chug-chug" when under load might have been the inspiration for the nursery story about the little engine that said, "I think I can, I think I can."

Fireman McKee once told of bringing one of these up out of the Noble County coal fields, hauling its full complement of loaded cars. Under full throttle the pop had opened. "For the heck of it," he said, "I gave her a few more scoops of coal." He then watched the needle on the steam gauge

Pennsylvania Lines

WEST OF PITTSBURGH

Office Copy

Eastern Division

TIME TABLE No. 7-B.

In effect 12.01 A. M., SUNDAY, APR. 5, 1914.

Superseding Time Table No. 7-A.

F. J. KRON,
Superintendent.

E. T. WHITER,
General Superintendent.

CHAS. WATTS,
General Sup't. of Passenger Transportation.

A. B. STARR,
General Sup't. of Freight Transportation.

BENJ. McKEEN,
General Manager.

Timetable for the Pennsylvania lines, 1914

climb on past the 150-mark, at which point he got cold feet, jerked open the fire door, and turned on the injector. He said he fully believed he could have blown her up. His engineer, one of the few mild-mannered ones of his breed, said, "I wish you wouldn't do that any more."

I was once privileged to watch a class R engine perform under dramatic circumstances. It was on a bitter-cold morning, with snow deep on the ground. My path homeward by speeder was blocked by a dead coal train, northward bound. Its engine, an H-6 had suffered a burst flue.

Standard procedure in this case required that the squirt hose be at once turned on the fire to save the crown sheet from buckling as the water drained from it. Within minutes it was a dead chunk or iron. A class R engine was on its way from Cambridge with orders to store this train on RA siding. I pulled my speeder off at the head end and walked to the caboose. The brakie was bleeding all cars of their last bit of air. No sticking brakes could be afforded here. In a short time the ambitious little engine arrived. No trainmaster or other official accompanied it and none was needed.

The dead train consisted of 2,700 gross tons, its maximum wintertime rating, but this did not take into account the weight of the now dead engine. The train rested on a slight upgrade of something like .025 percent. The class R's winter rating on the branch was an even two thousand tons. Its reputation would have to make up the difference. Opinion was divided among those present as to whether it could do the job or not.

First off, it coupled on and pulled the slack back, downgrade, until a trainman standing on the bank saw the ice break and fall away from the dead engine. Then the caboose and two hoppers of coal were cut off and shoved into Hager's spur, a short stockloading track nearby. This reduced the dead weight to be moved by some 230 tons. With all sanders running, the little engine was ready and seemed to say, "Let me at 'em." It rammed the coal train at 10 mph., then its throttle was opened full. With almost its last gasp of effort the train moved, and a cheer went up. The physics student would say inertia had been broken, and thus the contest was won.

Newscasting

When I first went to RA, it was, by the timetable, open only from ten P.M. to ten A.M. On November 1, 1916, RA was made a three-trick office, and I inherited first trick, seven A.M. to three P.M. — the first and only such trick I ever was to hold or wish to. However, it was these hours that permitted me to take on a bit of profitable "extra duty" one night.

Tuesday, November seventh, was to be national election day. President Wilson would run for a second term, opposed by Mr. Hughes. On the Sunday morning preceding this, I received an unusual call on my block wire: "RA, CS." This being Sunday morning and CS being Coshocton Western Union, the caller would have to be Mr. Foresman, my former boss.

First he questioned "GS?" When I said, "i," he asked if I could ground the line north for a minute. He wanted to talk privately with me. When I told him the ground was on, he said, "How would you like to come in and copy election returns for me Tuesday night? I will pay you sx5," which in English was five dollars. My answer was prompt. I said,

"Sure I will." He said, "Fine. You come in at eight o'clock and I will fill you in."

In 1916 the telegraph reigned as the world's fastest and most accepted news medium. There were some tickers about that gave stock quotations and play-by-play accounts of baseball games, but not very many people could congregate around a ticker to read its tape. Another five years would elapse before the infant radio outgrew its early gibberish of code and learned to speak and to broadcast the language. The telegraph was still tops and was the means by which an avid public would follow the progress of a national election.

The local chamber of commerce had arranged a street-corner election party, and the community was invited. A second-floor room above a saloon at the corner of Sixth and Main was rented and equipped for the occasion. A single morse line was run in here with the usual key, relay, and sounder, the latter in a resonator at the end of a swinging arm. The paper used was of a special transparency. It was in a roll, similar to today's paper towels. This fitted into a cardboard box, which was attached to and rode back and forth with the carriage of a standard-size Underwood typewriter.

The sending operator was in state election headquarters at Columbus. I would copy simultaneously with similar stations at Newark, Zanesville, Cambridge, Dover, and Mansfield. On a table fronting a window rested a magic lantern, the forerunner of today's slide projector. As each dispatch was completed, the roll of paper was given a few upward turns and scissored off by Mr. Foresman. He would then insert this in the magic lantern and the typed returns were projected in large characters onto a big white sheet attached to a building across Sixth Street.

The copying was continuous for about the first four hours. The sending was neither fast nor slow, but most precise. There were two sending operators at Columbus, and I could tell when one would spell off the other as his wrist tired.

At one point I was impelled to turn my head and look behind me, and there in a doorway stood my mother and father. We managed to exchange smiles. I was rather surprised at their presence. In order to get up here they had had to enter a stair door, down at street level, which was right next to the saloon door. This was probably the nearest they ever came to entering one of those places.

Once Mr. Foresman invited me to open my key and hop over to a window. The whole intersection was filled by people with upturned faces. We had a "good house." By four A.M. the crowd had greatly thinned. That many did remain was due to the fact that the race was still undecided. It was now evident that one state, California, would tip the scale one way or the other. And California, also having a close vote, had not been able to report its final count at that hour.

The agreement with the chamber of commerce had been to operate only from eight P.M. to four A.M. And so, leaving our audience to learn the final outcome from the next day's newspapers, I typed one final message for the magic lantern. It was "good night."

The War

April 6, 1917, arrived, and someone said that the sun rose that morning with blood on its face. We had been semiofficially in the European war for two years. Now we would be a full-fledged ally.

Two years earlier, on May 7, 1915, the Germans had shocked the world by torpedoing England's great liner the *Lusitania*, drowning more than twelve hundred people, including more than a hundred Americans. Following this, the Central Powers, as the enemy became known, introduced gas warfare, and fell even lower in world esteem. We entered with the idea of invading and winning, which, in my judgment, if we must have a war, is better than containing and prolonging.

This was a popular war by all common criteria, perhaps the last such we would know. We sang "Over There," "Pack Up Your Troubles," "Katy," and "Tipperary," among others. We bought Liberty Bonds or, if we couldn't afford these, War Savings Stamps at the post office. To the post office we brought our nutshells and dropped them in a big bag in the lobby. These would be charred, and the resultant charcoal became a filtering agent in the gas masks with which we must equip our doughboys. We would see sugar and gasoline rationed, and we had meatless Tuesdays.

At the old Mystic Theater in Coshocton, the following dialogue was heard between the straight man and a very slender comedian:

"What's your name?"
"Pickens."
"What's your first name?"
"Slim."
"Why is it people call you Tuesday?"
"Because I'm so meatless."

Prior to this time we had only thought that we were busy. Now, along with ballooning rail traffic, there would be competition for manpower with all the armed forces, plus the Merchant Marine. Topping all this, there followed the disastrous flu epidemic, plus the record cold winter of our busiest year. The extra list? None existed in any category of railroading for some two years. There was no rest for men or engines. Crews often worked sixteen-hour days. Passenger engines and crews as well hauled freight on Sundays.

President Wilson now appointed the honorable William G. McAdoo as Director General of Railroads, with a view to promoting more cooperation and less competition in this field. Bureaucracy we had then, too. Our railroad bought plain-faced cheap "clip" or message paper by the ton. It was as common as flies in a cow stable in summer and found everywhere. But now, under the new order, each sheet would be run through a printing press and come out with the heading:

UNITED STATES RAILROAD ADMINISTRATION
WASTE NO WORDS

One evening in mid-1917, Mr. Minto called me at home in Coshocton. He said that instead of my going to RA the next morning I was to meet him at Coshocton station at the departure time of the afternoon Wally Flier. That was all, and I was completely mystified. At the station next afternoon, Mr. Minto stood by, and with him was Mr. Harrold, railroad detective. Mr. Harrold was twice as big as Mr. Minto. Mr Minto told me that we were going to Warsaw Junction, where I was to take over second trick that day and thenceforward. I was puzzled but asked no questions.

At WJ we entered the station, where Mr. Minto notified the operator on duty that he was discharged, and Mr. Harrold notified him that he was under arrest. Thus, before the day was over, he was fired, arrested, charged, and fined— for thievery on a grand scale. Specifically, this was for opening an express package consigned to a Warsaw store and containing ten or so pairs of women's shoes. From these he had selected a pair that he thought his wife might wear. When it turned out that she couldn't, she gave them to a neighbor, saying nothing of where she had got them. This neighbor couldn't wear them either and in all innocence took them to the store to which they had been consigned to ask about a trade. When the storeman asked her where she had got them, she frankly told him.

This operator was a kleptomaniac of the first order.

When they moved out a couple of days later, the stash of stolen goods left behind was almost unbelievable. Among things brought back to the station were ten brand-new railroad lanterns, for which he had no earthly use, and a bundle of pencils about four inches thick. In a chicken house at the back of his property was left a ton or two of pipe, rod iron, flat iron, angle iron, and so forth, for which he also had no use.

I did not return to RA, but stayed on, as ordered, at Warsaw Jct. where, during the war and afterward, I worked 730 straight days, or two years, mostly on third trick, 11 P.M. to seven A.M. It was in no sense a promotion, but it did pay five dollars a month above the minimum. This was due in part to a small armstrong interlocking plant here, which governed the diamond where Akron Division's Dresden Branch (Killbuck to Trinway) crossed us.

During those summer seasons of 1917 and 1918, farmers, working hard to produce a bit more, found help with their harvests hard to come by. Women and children were helping on the farms, and several railroad employees, including myself, gave many hours of help in the fields. We helped with the hay. We shocked grain—once by moonlight. We helped thresh and fill silos. We cut corn and husked corn. We were paid a minimal wage, but mainly, I'm sure, we felt we were doing our extra bit to help the war effort. There were big posters about that said "FOOD WILL WIN THE WAR. DON'T WASTE IT." The hottest job I ever undertook was mowing back timothy hay in a tin-roofed barn in early July. The coldest was helping dry salt pork in an unheated outkitchen in November.

It was extremely cold around that winter's holiday season. Coshocton had planned a community Christmas tree and songfest in the Courtyard but canceled it because of the snow and bitter cold. There was an unofficial low of minus twenty one night.

The trackmen's tall tales now took on a winterish tone. One had been unable to blow out his lantern on coming in from doing the morning chores. He found the blaze to be frozen to the wick. Another's cow had given ice cream instead of milk. Still another "honest" fellow confessed he didn't know how cold it had been at his place. He had gone out on the porch to look at the thermometer, but no red was to be seen. He was turning away when he glanced back at a broom leaning against the wall, and there was the red mercury, halfway down the handle. There being no scale markings on the broom handle, he couldn't read the temperature. He was most regretful about this. Yet another trackman expressed his disgust with such weather and declared his intention to start doing as they did up in Holmes County when it snowed. "What do they do up in Holmes County when it snows⁰" he was asked. "Why," he said, "most of them just let it snow."

At Warsaw, I put in nine years among the most compatible of people, on and off the railroad.

Warsaw Junction

Warsaw was an incorporated village of less than a thousand. The Walhonding River ran at its feet, spanned by an old iron road bridge and by a railroad trestle. People walked across either of these. The town's backdrop was a low hill on which sat a red brick schoolhouse where the first ten grades were taught. It had no wealthy people and no poor ones. It had lots of everyday folks. It had two going churches. It had on its books a local option ordinance under the state's liquor code. In other words it was "dry," and it had an active WCTU chapter.

But Warsaw hadn't always been so quiet and respectable. It was an old town and had once been a port of call on the early Ohio Canal system. In my days, the canal bed was just a deep, dry ditch. But in former times it had been a busy thoroughfare. Its course ran close by the rear of business places along the main street's west side. Those had been rough and tough days, a feature commonly overlooked and lost in today's nostalgic memories. The canals both employed and attracted the rowdy and the lawless. When a

Station house at Warsaw Junction

boat was in town, there were apt to be bloody fights in the street or in any of its several saloons. If two boats were in, it was all the worse. Women dared not venture uptown. Law and order were nonexistent. In Warsaw, it was said, hell was only ten feet underground.

When I worked at Warsaw, there were still some old-timers around with vivid memories of those days. One tale they recounted with glee was how a local citizen had once emptied a crowded saloon, albeit he did this with no noble motive. His name was Ben. He was a hanger-on, a moocher, a pest. He was dour of nature and, after bumming a drink or two, quarrelsome of disposition. He was regularly thrown out of one dive after another.

One night a barkeep faced Ben with a bung starter and ordered him to get out and stay out. Ben answered by saying, "I'll get out, but I'll be back." This was regarded as Ben's usual bombast and paid no heed. However, a half hour later he was back. He yanked open the front door and onto the floor he rolled a bomb, yelling as he did so, "Run, you so-and-sos, run!" And slamming the door, he, too, ran.

Those within had but one way to run to save life and limb and that was out the back door and onto the narrow loading dock, from which each jumped, fell, or was pushed into the five-foot-deep canal.

The "bomb" turned out to be a twenty-inch length of farmer's drain tile, six inches in diameter, tamped with mud and with a short, burning fuse protruding one end. That was all. There was no explosive charge. Did Ben get a laugh from this? "Oh, no. Ben was never known to laugh. To him this was but a merited revenge."

In February of 1919, I was still the third trick man at Warsaw Jct. The press of war was over. The pace had eased, and this showed in people's faces. Tony Layman, the third trick coal dock attendant, and I now ran the whole shebang at night. He would attend to his preliminary duties at the dock, then come to the station and while away some time before my stove. Sometimes he took a nap. He was expert at firing the big cannon-type stove. He would clean out the ashes, then cram it full of soft Cambridge coal. Then he watched it burn awhile as he carefully regulated its draft. His fires could be counted on to burn steadily through the night—usually.

One night he came in, and instead of giving his usual greeting said, "I been to town today." "So?" I said. In answer he propped up two heavily shod feet so I could admire a pair of new boots. An army surplus store had opened up at Coshocton and he had come away with a pair of army hobnails. He was inordinately proud and pleased with his purchase and declared they would last him the rest of his life. They had been worn some and a bit of the mud of France, perhaps of Argonne Forest or of Belleau Wood still clung in seams and pockets. I voiced a passing thought regarding the former wearer. Had he come back, too? Had he taken off the boots, or had they been taken from his feet? This caused Tony to look at me strangely.

He went through his usual routine of loading the stove, then lay down on a desk. It was a short desk but if one placed a low-backed chair at its end on which to rest the heels, he could stretch out quite comfortably. The bottoms of his feet then would be a scant foot from the warm stove—quite cozy.

At the other end of the office I worked away at some midnight reports to be wired off to Cambridge and Akron. Almost an hour went by, and then I heard Tony stir and say something like, "Eeyow!" He slid his 175 pounds to the floor and as he did so he screamed as I had never heard a man scream. He made a wild dash for the outdoors, leaving two doors open behind him.

A nightmare, was my first thought, possibly engendered by my remarks concerning the former wearer of the boots. I peered out into the dim light and there was Tony, rapidly jumping rope on the snow-covered platform, or so it appeared, except that he had no rope. A measure of reason returned to me and I turned to examine the stove. A beautiful cherry-red streak several inches wide ran from fire pot to smoke collar just opposite Tony's footrest. Radiation and induction had combined to give him a class-one hotfoot.

When he at last came in, carrying the boots, Tony declared, "I'll never put them things on again." He did, of course. However, when he took off his socks the soles of his feet were, as he said, "red as a tom turkey's wattles."

In spring season, a work train from headquarters would visit the branch and stay a couple of weeks. It would lay up nights at Warsaw Jct., where coal and water were available. It consisted of a steam-powered clamshell, a few flats, and some drop-bottom gonds. It did ditching along the bluffs and some ballasting where needed. The ballasting material was at hand. This was engine cinder, a small mountain of which would accumulate here from one spring to the next. The clamshell, dipping into this one warm June day, uncovered a foot of gleaming white snow. Cinder was a by-product of the steam age that was widely used and is missed by the railroads, which now must buy and haul stone and gravel at high cost.

Young Frankie McClain, ambitious, strong, rosy-cheeked and aged about sixteen, was already a regularly employed trackman. He begged for and was given the additional job of night watchman for the work train's engine. This duty consisted of first cleaning the fire and thereafter only keeping it alive, and water in the boiler.

The engine parked on the station track near my back window. Periodically I would hear the clank of shovel or shaker bar, the hiss of the injector or the roar of the blower.

About daybreak one morning, I realized I had heard no sounds from the engine for some time. I went to investigate.

Frankie was not aboard. I opened the fire door. The fire amounted to a pile of red coals the size of a bushel basket. The steam gauge indicated about twenty pounds. I ran to the car inspector's shop. Here was Frankie, recumbent on the workbench, his rosy face a picture of blissful repose. I shook him awake and into action. Frankie said, "I'll surely get canned for this." "No you won't," I assured him. "I'll help you. We can get her hot." But I spoke with more assurance that I felt.

I ran to the office and asked for thirty minutes out. Nearby was a pile of discarded ties, partly rotted but dry. From the handcar shanty I brought a rail chisel and a spike maul. Using these as wedge and sledge we split several of the ties. From the car shop Frankie brought a bucket of black oil and we poured this on the pieces. These we then shoved into the firebox, followed by several shovels of nut coal. The fire blazed at once. A half hour later there was enough steam for the blower to become effective, and Frankie could smile. He still had a half hour before the crew would report for the engine. I, who had been helped often, had been able to give some help to one younger than myself.

I now had been a brasspounder for several years, yet still there were thing to be learned. I was to decide, for example, that an electrically charged wire was a means, or perhaps an aid, in transmitting telepathic messages. Such a message might come from a total stranger and be of no personal concern to me. And yet, on many occasions, especially in the still of night, a key would click open—the operator hesitating an instant as he formed in his mind what he meant to say, or whom he meant to call. Then, as his brain sent message to fingers, the same message would come to me. But if there was time to think or guess, the message would be lost.

No two fists on the morse key were alike. After some months of working with the same crew of about twenty-five on one trick, they took on an individuality as distinctive as the voice. The voice of fingers might be recognized before the sender otherwise identified himself. In fact, in all too many cases this would be the only voice of a fellow crafts-man that one would ever hear. Character and disposition were revealed in the same way. If one did eventually meet one of these fellow workers face to face, he knew pretty well beforehand what nature of person to expect.

This obvious individuality of each telegrapher's style, or "fist" as it was known in the trade, may have been my intro-duction to the concept that nature knows no duplicates. No two snowflakes, leaves, fingerprints, faces, voices, or fists on the morse key were alike. A fantastic thought!

The Murder Trial

At this time the Pennsy's old oil headlights were being replaced one by one with the electric type. Steam from the boiler was tapped to run a small generator just aft the smokestack. It generated much voltage and engine headlights were now brilliant and searching. These even transformed some habits of night railroading. Small animals that scurried along the track could now be picked out and identified.

An engine so equipped was hauling a southbound freight on the Wally. The time was around two o'clock of a cold and very dark morning in early March. Near the west end of Randles siding the fireman, having just shoveled in a fire, leaned out the gangway for a breath of air. He looked forward and a strange sight greeted him. More aptly, this was a mere glimpse. Just passing out of the headlight's beam he got a picture of an old man walking northward along the track. It was a picture in detail, however. The man was bearded, he wore an overcoat and a fur cap. He walked with a cane. In the other hand he carried an oilcan by the bail. It was a can of several gallons capacity.

From my station at Warsaw Jct., four miles north of this point, a second freight followed the one here mentioned by twenty minutes. The two trains were yarded in succession at Cambridge and the two crews gathered at the yard office to sign off and turn in time slips.

A member of the second crew, addressing himself to the first crew, said, "Did you fellows see that shanty afire at the north end of Randles?" The question brought blank looks from four of the crew, but the fifth member, the aforementioned fireman, evinced interest, and related what he had observed a hundred yards south of the point.

Several weeks later, three of these railroaders would appear in Coshocton County common plea court as witnesses for the State in its trial of one Riley Richesson for the murder of his nephew, Dave Richesson.

These two were of a subculture. Although natives of the community, they did not relate much with the responsible and industrious majority. They were largely illiterate, and self-consciousness stemming from this circumstance may have been responsible for their withdrawal.

The preceding fall, they had teamed up and moved into a vacated shanty on a narrow neck of ground between the railroad and the canal near the north end of Randles siding. The shanty seemed to be without ownership. There was no evidence, but it probably sat on the old towpath.

Riley, the uncle, was in his sixties; Dave, the nephew, was in his forties. Night and morning I rode by their place on my speeder. Largely through old Riley's industry, some repairs were made and a dozen chickens and some corn were acquired. Uncle and nephew had each saved some money from summer labors on area farms.

This teaming up may have seemed attractice in the beginning, but it soon grew into something else. Riley did the best he could to save and to stretch his small savings, but Dave was of different persuasion and squandered his. By midwinter he was broke. Then he borrowed from Riley. Later, he demanded small sums from his uncle. Still later he slapped the old man. Finally he told Riley he would put him in the canal, and he proceeded to chop a hole in the ice large enough for the purpose. Then, he fetched and leaned against the shanty a discarded steel brakebeam, which he had found along the railroad. it was five feet long and weighed about seventy pounds.

Perhaps Dave meant only to frighten his uncle further, but if so, he succeeded too well. When he came home quite late and probably drunk on this night of March, he tumbled into bed and was soon fast asleep. Riley, who only feigned sleep, slid quietly out on the other side. From two pegs on the wall he lifted down a 12-gauge shotgun and, poking this between the rods of their iron bed, shot Dave squarely in the top of the head.

Then, of course, he must cover up the deed. So beneath and on top of the bed he piled every combustible that he could find or think of. This included firewood and ear corn. Then the contents of their five-gallon oilcan were added. But there was only about a gallon in the can and it didn't seem quite enough. So he dressed himself fully—it was a cold morning, as already noted—and trudged down the track to Mr. Lincoln Frey's little store at the settlement of Randles. Mr. Frey sold kerosene from a barrel on the store porch. The barrel rested on a rack a couplr of feet above the floor and had an attached spigot. Here Riley refilled his can and returned home.

Soaking everything in sight, he at last tossed a match into

the interior. Then he returned to the settlement and pounded loudly on Mr. Frey's door, next to the store. When Mr. Frey answered the knock, Riley told him that the shanty was on fire and that he couldn't rouse Dave, who was asleep. Mr. Frey dressed hastily and started up the track. Riley chose to remain behind. Mr. Frey went only part way, far enough to see the roof collapse and send a fountain of sparks billowing a hundred feet into the black sky. He returned and opened the store door and told Riley he could stay inside the rest of the night. He had taken note that Riley was fully clothed and booted. On his home phone he roused the county sheriff.

Riley was arrested on suspicion and placed in the county jail. Later in the day, having been cooled by much water, the bed springs were lifted from the pyre. Dave's remains, resting thereon, were taken to the coroner's office. His weight had been reduced from 180 pounds to 30.

The coroner reported no evidence of foul play. The skull had burst but this, he said, was common when a body is consumed by fire. The sheriff was not convinced and a grilling that lasted most of two days was begun, while Riley stoutly maintained his innocence. But at last, having reached the limit of endurance, he confessed his role in the crime, while relating the circumstances that led to it.

At this time a funeral service for Dave was being conducted at Warsaw. The sheriff appeared there to halt burial and to return the remains to the coroner for further examination. This time, using a longer probe, the charge of shot, still compact, together with its wadding, was located deep in the neck.

My parents and I, like everyone else, followed the ghastly

details headlined in the morning *Tribune* and in the afternoon *Times Age*. The trial was an upcoming event, and the last thing we imagined was that I would be caught up in its backwash. But one day my mother answered a knock at the door and there stood a man wearing the badge of a deputy sheriff. He asked if I was at home. Ma told him yes, but added that I worked nights and was sleeping. "Very well," he said. "When he wakes up, you hand him this and tell him to come to the courthouse and talk to the prosecuting attorney." He handed her an official-looking document bearing the State of Ohio Seal and the word *subpoena*.

She was frightened into further grayness of hair. She paced the floor for about ten minutes, then came and wakened me. I was probably no less frightened. I dressed hurriedly and ran to the courthouse and there inquired for the prosecutor. This gentleman (I believe he was Mr. Leech) smiled, apparently at my anxious face. He asked me whether, at my station, I had a record of the departure time of the two freights, some crew members of which were to testify at the trial. I told him I had such a record and he instructed me to be in court with it the day after tomorrow. This, he explained, might serve to establish the time of the alleged crime. I assured him I would be on hand. Then I ran back home to reassure my mother.

And so I was at the courthouse for the trial, but not in the courtroom. Being a witness, I must not be allowed to listen to other witnesses. For two days I cooled my heels in the sheriff's office. Then the prosecutor came and excused me, saying that my testimony would not be required. I collected a small sum in witness fees and left.

The next day I was back as a spectator. I heard summations before the jury by the prosecutor and by Mr. Durand, the court-appointed attorney for Riley.

The trial was conducted by the learned judge James Glenn. Judge Glenn, incidentally, was not noted as a speaker, but in the matter of the written legal opinion he was an accepted genius. In his summation, the defense attorney was rapped to order by the judge, who said, "Mr. Durand, you have several times referred to your client as a person of below average mentality. I would remind you that there is no such thing as an average human mentality. The human mind in its scopes, its reaches, and its powers varies as much as does the human countenance, and there have never been two people who looked alike." (The quotation is from memory.)

Perhaps it was these words that introduced me to the idea that nature spawns no duplicates.

The prosecutor demanded a verdict of first-degree murder, based on the theory that if Riley had escaped the common bed, he could also have escaped the house and the vicinity to save his own life, without resort to murder.

First degree the jury voted, but they added the recommendation of mercy. In so doing, I imagine that they had a two-fold motive, the second of which was punishment. The primary one, I believe, was a common wish that Riley might spend his remaining years where he would be safe, where he would be warm in winter, and where there would always be enough to eat. At the London, Ohio, prison farm, these things could be had.

High Jinks and Humor

The advent of another warm April would now help folks forget the ugliness of the March past and its preoccupation with snow, ice, cold, and murder. Mushrooms were beginning to sprout up and down the valley, and this subject was ever so much more inviting. It marked the coming of another spring. The imaginative trackmen rose to the occasion with spirit and inventiveness and with a creativity and ingenuity that tested credulity.

One had filled a sack in no time with the aid of his bird dog, which he had trained to "point" them. Another had stumbled onto a patch where mushrooms sprouted so rapidly they were literally jumping out of each other's way. He had only to set down his basket among them, and in no time it was filled. Still another related, with some regret, how he had passed up and left standing one of the biggest mushrooms he had found that day. When duly asked the reason for this, he explained that it was because of his unduly kind nature. "It was drizzling rain," he explained, "and when I got closer I could see this old cow standing beneath it in the dry. She was contentedly chewing her cud and lazily tossing her tail and, well, I just didn't have the heart to drive her off."

This was a sort of yarn to end yarns, a cap sheaf as it were. It brought stares and silence, until one listener recovered sufficiently to fire a parting shot: "Are you sure that wasn't bull?" he asked.

One mild April day, alive with the promise of spring, a soft shower had passed our way, enough to dampen the clothing of the four-man section gang. They had a rule, unwritten and ill-defined, that they be not required to work in the rain; thus they exercised some latitude in determining what constituted a rain. To work in damp clothes might, of course, lead to pneumonia, so they felt justified in retiring to the freight house attached to the nearby depot to dry out.

While doing so, what better way to pass the time than a little four-handed game of cinch? They sat down in a circle on the plank floor. One produced a tobacco can from which he shook a dog-eared deck of cards. Another announced, "This is where friendship ceases," and the others laughed. The game at once got under way. They played not for money but for the much higher stakes of pride, honor, and glory. They played in deep earnest. They were oblivious to their surroundings.

A fifth member of the gang now showed up. This man was a member only inasmuch as he worked under the same foreman, but his status here was that of the uninvited guest. He was the first-trick coal-dock attendant and as such his pay scale was a bit higher than that of the others. This definitely excluded him from the circle, and there was nothing he could do about it.

There were other things he might do, though. The south-bound package local had gone and the agent had pulled a baggage truckload of flour in fifty-pound paper bags into the freight house. A little tear in one of these had allowed a small conical heap of its contents to spill onto the truck bed. The coal-dock man disappeared into the office and returned with a sheet of newspaper. Going to the truck he scraped the spilled flour onto this. It amounted to a couple of pounds.

A tall ladder stood in a far corner. Mr. J. B. Clark, the agent, climbed this once a month to store records above the ceiled part of the building. The frieght-house part was not ceiled, only the exposed joists crossed overhead.

The coal-dock man quietly ascended this ladder carrying the newspaper sheet by its four corners. With one hand holding to the rafters above his head, he walked the joists until he was directly over the seated card players. Then, from fifteen feet, he released his bomb. It landed with quite a smack. It was a direct hit amidships.

The four heads went up as one and the four mouths puffed away flour in unison. The four damp jackets, which had been a faded blue, were now white.

I had observed the melodrama thus far and was duly curious as to what the next act would be, but I had business that took me elsewhere just then. Moreover, if I remained, I stood to be charged as an accessory after the fact, inasmuch as I had been a silent witness to it all.

Another trackman who became a friend was Bill Wilson, who had lost an arm while at work on the railroad. As part of his settlement with the company, he had been promised a lifetime job suitable to his capability. This promise was faithfully kept. When I knew him best, he was tunnel watch-man at Tunnel Hill, south of Warsaw Jct. on the Dresden Branch. He pumped a speeder back and forth and had rigged a brush on the front end to clean snow from the rail when necessary. On arrival at his job, he walked the tunnel, looking for fallen rock. He also walked it after each train.

The loss of his arm had not affected Bill's disposition, which was sunny, nor his chuckle, which was more of a "tee-hee." He would demonstrate for you how he laced and tied his shoes, filled and lit his pipe, and wound his watch, holding the latter in his mouth. He had a cousin in the vicinity of the same name. The two were distinguished as "Windy Bill" and "One-armed Bill."

One did not think of him as a scholar, but as an explorer of the timbered, hilly region that was Tunnel Hill he had no peer. Between trains there was ample time for this. In season, Bill brought home with him mushrooms, berries, and nuts. He was handy with a light-weight single-barrel shotgun and in fall would bang his quota of squirrel, rabbit, and an occasional young groundhog. He had found and developed for use a spring of what must have been the coldest water ever to flow from the ground. Many berry pickers and hunters visited this. It is quite probable that they still do, though Bill, the railroad, and the tunnel are long gone.

Once Bill captured a four-foot blacksnake of which he meant to make a pet. But this was not to come about. He had a little shanty that sat on a leveled area called a shelf, cut from the sloping approach to the tunnel some fifteen feet above track level. It was reached from the track by steps dug into the shale face. To the shanty Bill brought his snake. He brought it milk from home, and it was content to remain indoors as long as the door remained shut.

Bill's immediate boss was the section foreman. The relationship between these two was a bit less than cordial. It was said the foreman had had something to do with Bill's losing the arm. One day Bill saw the foreman approaching the shanty and he quickly lifted the snake to a shelf above the one bench the place afforded. The foreman entered and sat down, leaving the door open as he chided Bill for having it closed on such a nice day.

From the corner of his eye Bill saw the snake edging over the brink. Then down it came in a free fall across the boss's shoulders. He shot straight up as though catapulted, his head striking the shelf above, bringing it down along with its accumulation of cans, lanterns, papers, dust, et al. Bill said he tried all four sides of the shanty before finding the door. Then, in terror, he was gone.

A bit later Bill thought he should go see what had become of the man. He hurried to the edge of the stony shelf and there saw evidence that the boss had disregarded the steps and had slid or rolled to the bottom. He was nowhere in sight. Bill said, "I guess he was still runnin'. Tee-hee!"

The snake? "I never saw it again," he said.

We made many boners, and a history of the brass-pounder would be remiss if it did not record some of these. Some were real and some had the tone of fable. A few were serious, but the funny ones are best remembered.

The letters *i* and *o* along with *l* and *t* were pitfalls for the tyro. The *i* is two staccato dots; the *o* is two dots separated by a fractional interval. The *l* is a long dash, the *t* is a short dash.

A bridge inspector stopped in at the nearest telegraph office to file an urgent message to the superintendent. When received, it read: "Found a lion under bridge 16 unsafe for traffic." The superintendent probably said "Bosh" or words to that effect and asked to have the message repeated. When this was done it read: "Foundation under bridge 16 unsafe for traffic."

Once the conductor of a troop train, en route from Fort Leonard Wood to Norfolk, threw off a message at a wayside station near Xenia addressed to the station master at Columbus, Ohio. The message as copied down read: "Please have 100 tons mold pope tobacco delivered our commissary car your station." The operator at DK in Union Station, Columbus, was an old hand. He had heard them all. He said to himself, "Hmmm." Judging from the message's point of origin, the train might be only minutes away. On his own responsibility he hastily rewrote the message to read "100 tins mild pipe tobacco" and dashed off to the stationmaster's office to deliver it in person.

Another comes from Western Union's annals. A branch plant manager, together with his wife, had gone to headquarters in a distant city to attend a New Year's Eve dinner, to be followed by a ball. Trouble had developed at the home plant and the man left in charge had sent a panicky telegram to his boss which, upon receipt, read in part: "Hurry back at once don't wait for the batt."

Special Duty

Came spring of 1922 and I was furloughed for the first and only time. My division, being primarily a coal hauler serving the union fields of Guernsey, Noble, and Washington counties, was virtually shut down by a miners' strike. "So what?" was my attitude. It would be a relief to escape the monotony of third trick. The farmer's hours were sun to sun, but he ate well and he slept soundly at night. At this time of year a job as farmhand could be had for the asking. It was merely a question of where I should apply. The wage would be the same anywhere. This was a dollar a day and keep.

This matter of "keep" had the most appeal. It would doubtless be lavish wherever I chose to go. Two miles up the river lived a congenial farmer whom I knew, so I would go there to ask about a job. "Sure," he told me. "Come in the morning if you can and you can go right to work."

At this point his wife interposed a pertinent question. "Do you have a pair of rubber boots?" When I told her no, she said, "I'll tell you what. You go get a pair and you can come for supper and stay all night." Her question and proposition were canny and to the point. Boots, as I learned, were pulled off on the back porch before one entered the house.

Early the next morning, with team and wagon, I commenced hauling manure from a big barn where twelve steers, four horses, and four milk cows had spent the winter. At early bedtime I would fall asleep on a fifteen-inch-thick husk mattress and seldom stir until awakened early by inviting odors rising from the kitchen—the best possible alarm clock. I felt great and was thoroughly enjoying myself.

This farmer had a boat and I was free to use it to do a little fishing. He also had an automobile of which he was proud and which he used sparingly. He housed it in an old log barn, which was unused and without windows. He had bought a two-gallon can of motor oil and added a bit from time to time to the engine. When the can was at last empty, he tossed it outdoors into the daylight. Then he followed and read the inscription thereon. It said, "Bickman's Concentrated Sheep Dip." The car had made no complaint. He was now even more proud of it, and he still had the two gallons of oil.

I had been a month at this job when one morning the farmer's wife summoned me to the house to answer a long-distance telephone call. She said Akron was calling. This must be a mistake, I thought. I knew no one in Akron. I had never been there.

But it was Akron. It was Mr. J. W. Murphy, division operator of Pennsy's Akron Division. "Will you come up here and help us out?" was his question. "We need a message man for AK. The place is swamped. We have everybody working. I have Mr. Minto's permission to take you on as a borrowed man."

One didn't hear the term Akron Division used much. More commonly it was known to all as the CA&C. In years gone by it had been the Cleveland, Akron & Columbus Railway Company, later to be absorbed by the Pennsylvania. The coal strike that had flattened my division had served to boom the CA&C's freight. At Columbus they were being offered coal in unprecedented amounts, coming from nonunion fields of states to the south.

"The job pays eighty cents an hour," Mr. Murphy continued. "You can work every day. A good mill and a bug are provided. How soon can you be here?" My initial reaction was a wish that he hadn't found me. I was doing just fine where I was. Then I considered the pay figure, which would be several cents more per hour than I had made before. And after all, maybe I shouldn't refuse to help out. Mr. Murphy was a man of good repute in the region, and he was in a bind. I told him I would be in on No. 605 the next day.

Next morning at Warsaw Jct. I boarded the Trinway to Millersburg mixed local (passenger and freight) and changed to CA&C's No. 605 at the latter place. At 11 A.M. I debarked at Akron Union Station and inquired where to find CA&C's division office. When I entered it and stopped in a doorway marked Division Operator, a big man with snow-white hair arose from a desk and approached me with extended hand. He called me by name and said, "I'm Murphy." I wondered afterward how he knew who I was.

He said, "Here, let me have your coat and cap. I'd be glad if you'd go to work right away. AK is hours behind and the superintendent has been riding me to get this cleared up. If you will work till four P.M., when second trick comes on, I will allow you a full day."

He led me into the message room. The trappings were familiar. I plugged in a wire and tested the bug for feel. It was set quite fast and I cut this down some, as I knew my wrist would not be loose again for a day or so. Within five minutes of entering the place I was at work, spitting them out and pounding them down. I would work here with GO Pittsburgh, DK Columbus, and the RD Cleveland, plus all stations up and down the line. I tackled about a two-inch stack of send stuff in a wire basket. I had made little impression on this when four P.M. came, as clerks from all over the building kept adding to it. Once I turned away from the mill and found two candy bars at my elbow. I presumed they were meant for me.

I worked at AK sixty six days hand-running, but on all the tricks.

The train dispatcher's office was up two steps and through an open doorway. His prime communication was now the telephone. His receiver was a loudspeaker. One night an excited male voice came in on this and shouted, "DI, DI! Listen. I'm on the Erie. I tell you I'm on the Erie!" The dispatcher talked him down to earth and got a lucid account of who, what, and where. He was the engineer of a Pennsy light engine backing from South Akron engine house, bound for Cleveland. When his engine arrived in front of Akron's Union Station, he found to his dismay that he was on the Erie Railroad's main southbound track. His position was indeed precarious. It could be likened to the soldier in battle who awakens suddenly to the fact that he is behind enemy lines.

Just south of Union Station was JO Interlocking Plant, where the two double-track lines crossed in a long maze of intricate or "puzzle" switches and frogs. A brakeshoe had lodged in one of these and diverted the engine to the wrong pair of rails. The only solution was for Erie to provide a pilot who would guide the engine back to Barberton's transfer track where it could be switched back to its own railroad, to try once again.

Working with GO, one day early July, I experienced another instance of telepathy between telegraphers. I began to copy a message with the dateline Cambridge, Ohio. Following the address, the sending operator's eye would naturally fall to the first few words of the message proper. When this occurred, I "read" these words along with him. Even if he had failed to send the message, I could confidently have typed out the first three words. They were, "Instruct operator Sanders . . . " To be sure, the dateline plus the fact that I knew the coal strike to be over might have been clues to the message's content, but not necessarily to its exact first words.

This was my order to return home. I took it in person to Mr. Murphy. He was not ready to let loose of me and said that if I would elect to stay he would put me on his roster as of the day I had begun here. I told him, "No thank you!" I was more than ready to return to the "land of milk and honey."

It was nice to be back in the Walhonding Valley, where faces, voices, and aromas were familiar, sounds and sights more acceptable. The corn that was being planted when I left was now "high as an elephant's eye." Nights were quiet. Summer apples were ripening and spring rabbits were half grown.

There would be about three more of these golden years.

Goodbye to the Wally

Looking back now, the lean period in the summer of 1922 seems to have marked a turning point in the fortunes of the Walhonding branch and of the parent Marietta Division as a whole. First to fall under the executioner's axe (with some outside help) would be the beloved Wally Flier. My last ride on the little train is memorable. I boarded it at Coshocton. When out of town, I walked through to the baggage car to chat with the ever-voluble baggageman, Alva Wichert. I saw at once that Alva was troubled. His customary gusto was lacking. He shook a warning finger under my nose. He said, "You won't be taking many more rides with me." I asked why not, and he told me.

That morning, in order to sign the trainmen's register in the baggage room of Mansfield's passenger station, he had had to climb over a waist-high stack of U.S. mail of all classes for Coshocton. On hand was the assistant trainmaster, who officially notified the crew that they were to load none of this—not this morning nor on any future morning. Presumably, Coshocton would receive this mail some twenty hours later than common at the end of a 325-mile haul by way of Pittsburgh, as against the usual 63 miles via the Wally.

However, there was method to the railroad's madness. By being denied this mail, the Wally Flier would now incur a loss of revenue. This would be evidence the railroad could present to the State Utilities Commission in Columbus some months later when they would ask, and receive, permission to discontinue the train. This, in some circles, is known as kicking a man after he's down.

This was my introduction to a process that still continues. The railroads, by a number of means including trickery and deception, were sloughing off local freight and passenger service in favor of the more lucrative long-haul freight business. I was destined during my forty-some remaining years on the Pennsy to witness the sorry spectacle of the railroads abandoning service to the public, in favor of sheer profit, just as fast as state commissions and the ICC could be persuaded to go along.

The Wally Flier was an intrastate train, one originating and terminating within the state of Ohio. Thus it existed and operated under the aegis and by the sufferance of the aforementioned State Utilities Commission.

A public notice appeared in local newspapers advertising an appeal before this commission by the Pennsylvania Railroad Company to ask for the Wally Flier's discontinuance. Pursuant to this, a protest delegation was formed in one of the small communities up the valley. This group was on hand at the capitol on the appointed day and hour to ask for a voice in the hearings. When its spokesman was given the floor, a railroad attorney asked him, "How did you good people get down to Columbus?" The spokesman answered, "We chartered a bus." "That will be all, thank you!" said the attorney. And that, indeed, was all as far as their protest was concerned.

Coming events cast their shadows before them and the next move by railroad management would be the dissolution of the Marietta Division as such. There would be no more division headquarters at Cambridge. Its two component parts would continue to function, however. Its main stem, the Dover to Marietta section, would fall under Cleveland Division's wing. The Wally Branch would fall under that of Eastern Division. Operators were given the option of going either place. Under this circumstance they would take with them their accumulated seniority as well as pass and pension rights.

My choice was made before it was offered. Small factors sometimes influence major decisions, and this would apply to me. I knew they ran a whole flock of the glamorous K-4 engines up on Eastern Division. On still nights I had often heard their eerie moaning whistle from as far as twenty miles down the Walhonding River. Carried this far over water it was an enchanting sound, which brought a pleasurable shiver. One might describe it as something between the mournful howl of the coyote and the siren song of the Lorelei. I would go the the Eastern Division—Pittsburgh to Crestline on the New York to Chicago line. This was the "big time."

In 1925, after I had exercised my last option on the Wally, I took the long step. I bumped in on second trick at Lakeville cabin. I would start as low as I could and feel my way along. Directly across the tracks from me at my new site was milepost 150, which assured me that I was that far from headquarters at Pittsburgh, where I knew not just how I was being received.

The cabin stood on the bank of Lake Odell, which covered something more than a hundred acres. It was a popular resort in summer. Just up the track stood a huge icehouse belonging to the railroad. For many years ice had been harvested from the lake and stored here under saw-dust. In summer it was shipped by carload to Canton, which was a re-icing point for refrigerator cars from the west. The railroad now operated an artificial ice plant there and the cavernous old icehouse was abandoned, except for its bats.

One night a boy of the community was visiting me when we felt the cabin shake. He went outdoors to see who the joker might be. Then he hollered for me to come out. There was a bright moon. The lake was frozen over to a depth of about an inch. Now, for as far as we could see, this was broken into pieces the size of a man's hand. There had been an earth tremor. His reaction was, "That's going to play heck with the skating."

Here the railroad was double track, with automatic signals for trains moving with the current of traffic. The train ahead set the pace for the train following, as the former shorted electrical circuits in the two rails. It was, further, an effective system, inasmuch as its signal would indicate "stop and go" automatically when activated by a broken rail, by a switch not properly set, or by an obstruction.

A train moving against the current of traffic would operate under the manual block rules, with which I was entirely familiar. Two siding switches and the two switches of a trailing crossover (all hand operated) were in my charge, and I had been extremely careful to bring along my old switch key, fastened to a long leather thong.

Communications here were primarily by telephone, but there were two stand-by morse lines. I would learn that there was a sprinkling of block operators here who did not telegraph, and these were known as "bell ringers."

Some two years later, sadly, I was to read in the paper that the Muskingum Valley Flood Control people would build an earthen dam across the Walhonding River. It would be located some two miles upstream from the village of Nellie. It would be called Mohawk Dam. This would place the dam at about milepost 15 on the Wally, and I visualized the site with sadness. If there had been any lingering hope of return, it died here.

The Saga of the K-4

Here at Lakeville, my little office stood beside the path of Pennsy's fabulous Blue Ribbon fleet, which included the Manhattan, the Liberty, the Red Arrow, the General, and the Broadway. All were hauled at great speed and with effortless motion by the graceful and powerful K-4.

If the homely little class R engine was the willing slave, the sleek K-4 was at the other end of the social scale. She was the queen, the one with the class and the aplomb. She both looked and acted the part. She appeared always conscious of her station. She would pick her way daintily across the turntable and up the ladder track. She would wait patiently while a trainman righted a switch in her path. I once got hold of an engineer's manual and therein discovered the secret of her poise and demeanor. Her full name although she never insisted on its use, was "K-4 Pacific." Pacific means peaceful, and she would live up to this.

Unless one knew her, one might never guess that she concealed 205 pounds of steam pressure in her boiler or

that, with her 80-inch drivers, she could and did roll a passenger train at a hundred miles an hour when called on to
do so. She was entrusted with hauling presidents and visiting dignitaries about the country. A presidential special
train was commonly preceded over the road by a pilot
engine that maintained an exact ten-minute lead. It was the
K-4, too, that moved major league baseball clubs and their
retinues of reporters over the system.

On an afternoon of the late 1920s a Chicago lady of station and means, named McCormick, missed connections
with the Broadway Limited out of that city. She shook a
ticket clerk out of his poise by demanding a special train to
New York City. Further, it must arrive there coincidentally
with the already departed Broadway.

It is not probable that this would occur in any other
American city. Chicago was and is a lusty place, where the
pioneer spirit still raises its head now and then and imagination is apt to be followed by action. They're rambunctious
out that way.

The railroad had been challenged. The system was
alerted and wheels began turning. A suitable Pullman, with
dinette, was switched out of the coach yard while staff and
provisions were assembled. The most available train and
engine crews were ordered out. A high-wheeled K-4 was
tied on and the train precisely spotted for the lady and her
small entourage to step aboard.

Probably before they were seated, the train moved out, a
bit more than an hour behind the Broadway—which train,
be it noted, had the fastest of all schedules between the two
cities. Standby engines waited at scattered points. This bob-
tailed special passed my station near midnight, some thirty-

On Time, *a painting by Grifteiter, depicting the Pennsylvania's K-4 engine hauling the Golden Arrow across the flatlands of Indiana at dusk on a winter night*

five minutes behind the Broadway. The next night we learned it had glided into New York's Penn Station right on Broadway's tail.

The K-4's grateful owners have enshrined old 1361 on Horseshoe Curve near Altoona. Her drivers no longer roll, there's no steam in her boiler, her mellow whistle is mute. She may be admired as she sits there, cold and immobile, yet still dignified in line and in pose. But her forte was action. The most graceful and nimble of dancers, sitting in a chair, may be passed unnoticed. It is on stage that they thrill and move great audiences to applause. But 1361 will go on sitting there, sitting and brooding, as do many other veterans of her romantic and virile era.

I prefer to remember the K-4 by a painting on my wall, a convincing action portrayal by a kindred soul by the name of Grifteiter. It pictures the 5411 hauling the Golden Arrow across the flatlands of Indiana at early dusk of a winter night. There is to be another section, for she's "carrying green" on her boiler head, both the flags and the lights being dimly visible in the twilight. Judging by the way she's kicking up the snow to the tops of her maroon cars, I have a feeling that she's doing nearer ninety than the allowable eighty. Maybe I will pad her time by a minute so she won't be called up on the carpet when she gets to Fort Wayne. My painting is entitled *On Time*.

The Benedict

In 1925 I moved from Lakeville to Burton City, a tiny community some miles to the east. In 1927 I married Irene Lennon.

She was Kansas born. Out there corn grows high, wheat flourishes in golden abundance, sunflowers grow everywhere, and virtue thrives the year around. There it is an element of life. At age 11 Irene lost her mother, and thereafter the Lennon family returned to Coshocton County, Ohio, which had been the family seat, and it was there I met her.

In Coshocton she graduated from high school and thence, with little more than determination to back her, worked her way through teacher's training at Ohio Northern University In her second year there she was joined by her cousin, Polly Hall, and the two roomed together. Today, when they get together and reminisce, all they seem to recall of the experience is laughing. It seems they laughed at this, that, everything, and nothing. Then they laughed because they didn't know what they had been laughing about.

Irene still enjoys life and loves to laugh. But as she matured, I decided that her greatest virtue was a strong sense of morality, principle, and responsibility, and these were probably the subjects she best taught her charges. She has firm ideas of what is right and what is wrong and an ability to impart these to others by example.

Teaching, however, did not fill her life to the exclusion of other worthy pursuits. Over the years she has become a top-notch seamstress and tailor of both imagination and skill. Furthermore, she cooks and bakes with the best of them.

To us were born two daughters, Jane and Sandra, who have brought us only happiness and pride. Jane is now a much-loved registered nurse with a family of her own. Sandra is a writer of skill, living in the East.

One of the nicest things about Irene, speaking here in a "relative" sense, was her uncle, Ad Clark, a Coshocton County farmer and dairyman and a master of wit and repartee. Today, with a good agent, he might make a fortune on the stage with much less effort. One sometimes laughed at his serious face in anticipation of what he might say.

The papers were currently headlining the trial of a man charged with the particularly heinous murder of a young woman. Uncle Ad's young hired hand asked him, "Don't you s'pose he'll get the galluses?" Ad's prompt rejoinder was, "You can't tell, it might be a suspendered case."

On another occasion, several guests were gathered about his dinner table. The main course was chicken and dumplings—most delicious. The four men of the party were seated together—Uncle Ad, Irene's father, Ed, her brother,

John, and myself. My father-in-law, patently with the aim of priming Uncle Ad, asked him, "What do you reckon ailed this chicken, Ad?" In confidential and pseudo-earnest tone Ad replied, "I really don't know, Ed. She drooped around here for a couple o' days and then this mornin' I found her dead out on the manure pile." The other diners were women who chattered without pause and, fortunately, this banter didn't reach their ears.

The 1930s

The depression era descended upon us, and in 1931 I narrowly escaped being furloughed again but managed to cling to the extra list for some two and a half years. During this time I got in days at all the block-interlocking stations and message centers from Leetonia at milepost 63 to Toledo Jct. at milepost 182. I put in more time traveling to and from these jobs than I did working.

We had moved from Burton City a couple of miles west to Orrville, and in 1932 our first daughter, Jane, was born. I cashed in a life insurance policy that I had bought through my father and gleaned some eight hundred dollars from this. We rented a neat little house on Fair Street in Orrville for eighteen dollars a month.

The J. M. Smucker Company (now world famous for its foods and condiments), helped us out. Mr. Chauncey Hostetler, son-in-law of the elder J. M. Smucker and husband of the Smucker daughter, Winna, was then the overseer of two large Smucker farms, one at the west edge of town and the other three miles out north. On each farm was an apple orchard of about thirty acres. Here, for a minimal wage, I could put in as many days or hours as I could manage.

In the spring of 1931, Mr. Hostetler and I, with the assistance of Jerome and Gordon, his two young sons, set about spraying each of these orchards with an insecticide. Following this, we sprayed all the trees in Crown Hill Cemetery, by contract with the town. In the fall, with much other help, we began picking apples. Then, with team and wagon, I hauled apple pomace (which we called pummys) from the apple-butter factory to the tillable acres of the two farms, where they had some value as mulch and fertilizer. Later, I painted the tin roof of the huge barn on the farm out north.

Following this, it was time to make cornmeal for the coming winter. In this the Hostetlers followed a unique method: Selected ears were hand shelled, then roasted in the oven to a rich brown before being taken to the mill to be ground. We were given a big bag of this, amounting to several pounds. With fall at hand, I was set to work cleaning up a five-acre woodlot on the farm next to town. I bought me a five-foot, one-man crosscut saw, which I still have and use occasionally. In this work I was allowed the use of team and wagon to haul home the more burnable of this wood. This I dumped into the cellar. With this wood, along with some coal, we heated the house one winter.

But the smaller stuff (brush) was not wasted. This I used early the next spring when I was permitted to tap a number of sugar maples. Working alone and putting in many twelve-hour days, I finally produced seven gallons of maple syrup, using a huge iron kettle. The long hours may be understood when it is explained that the ratio of sap to syrup was about thirty-three to one. That is, thirty-three gallons of sap were boiled down to produce one gallon of syrup. The Hostetlers would accept only one gallon of this. I shipped one gallon to my folks. The rest was ours.

In 1934, I at last held a regular job again. This was a relief job out west, where I would work three days a week at Erie Crossing, Mansfield, and two out at Toledo Jct., seven miles on west. We had no car then. I roomed at Mansfield and walked two days a week between there and Toledo Jct.

In 1936 daughter Sandra was born.

Then, in 1937, I got a big break, or so I thought at the time. In that year, operator Denver Johnson and I were invited to Pittsburgh to break in as train dispatchers. While doing this we would be paid the rate of the respective operator's jobs that we held. After two months in Pittsburgh, however, we were sent back home, in an economy move. The next year we were recalled.

Denver went, but I did not respond this time. I said, "No, thank you."

Over and over in the year past I had reminded myself of the words and logic of dispatcher Bill Snyder while in Pittsburgh in 1937. Bill told me, quite soberly, that had he had things to do over he would have remained at home in Canton, and grown up with his two sons. And I was to recall that years earlier I had wisely left Western Union rather than face the prospect of a future job and a future life in the city. I was then, and I remain, strictly "small town."

From my Mansfield–Toledo Jct. job I returned home once a week on No. 22, the Manhattan, due in about 6:30 P.M. At this hour, daughter Jane, aged five, would be allowed to take the hand of daughter Sandra, aged one,

Don Sanders at work in the Orrville interlocking tower of the Pennsylvania Railroad. From <u>Orrville Courier Crescent</u>, December 16, 1965

and walk about a block and a half and wait there at the street corner for me to show up. While I was yet half a block away I would see them start jumping up and down and hear them squeal in delight. Once I brought them each a small present. Sandra's was a little fuzzy white rabbit with long ears and pink eyes. She accepted this, then walked to the curb and dropped it in the gutter. I will never forget this, nor quite understand it. Apparently she wished only to see me and didn't want to be bothered with any rabbit.

In 1938 I latched onto the second-trick operator's spot at Orrville, and I was through roaming. I was to remain on this job until retiring in 1965.

Heroes and Goats

Some in our craft became goats and others heroes. Some managed to qualify in both classes.

Oscar, as a young operator, was on third trick at Cambridge Scales where his duties included weighing coal. A yard engine would shove a cut of loaded cars over his floodlit scale at slow speed, during which interval it was his job to jot down each car's initial, number. and gross weight. A heavy cover of snow blanketed the outdoors one night. Sounds from without were muffled, and because of this a cut of cars crept onto the scale without his hearing it. When he looked out the window the lead truck of the first car was just passing off the scale and hence could not be weighed.

Oscar could have sounded a horn and stopped the movement, but he decided against it. He would estimate this one. It was a PRR H-21 hopper with load rounded up a bit higher than common. He had been on this job long enough to judge by sight when a coal car was overloaded and by about how much. So he lumped this one off as 104 gross tons and 74 tons net, not a serious overload but one he thought might satisfy the critical eye of some car inspector along the way.

When this car reached destination, the consignee was billed freight charges for 74 tons of horse manure (intermixed with bedding straw) with which it had been loaded at a valley mine stable. It is probable that 15 tons would have been a generous guess had Oscar known the car's contents.

This chicken came home to roost and Oscar was given a reprimand, which meant that he performed that night's work for no pay. He would have been glad to accept the reprimand and let it go at that had it not been for the ribbing that followed, and continued to follow him, for the next year and a half.

At this time Oscar was on second trick at Haddon cabin on the Wally. He sat at his table one afternoon, momentarily expecting No. 909, the afternoon passenger train, to be reported into his block. Suddenly all three of his wires clicked open and were dead. This was a startling circumstance, which might have serious meaning. One of these, the block line, ran only the length of the branch. Thus, the probability was that this simultaneous break of all three was on the branch itself. The implication was ominous. It might indicate a wreck, a landslide, a fallen tree. At his switchboard he grounded each wire south and each went closed, thus the break was in that direction. He walked out on the track for a look down that way.

What he saw now chilled his blood. The whole facade of Stricker's Bluff, a third of a mile down the track, was changed. A tall sentinel pine, which had stood at its brow, was now down near track level, where it pointed horizontally out over the river.

He was long legged was Oscar, and he took off like the

frightened antelope of legend. Out of breath, he pawed and clawed his way over the mass of rock and rubble, then went on running. On the point of the curve, some five poles or five hundred feet beyond, he flagged No. 909, approaching at 40 mph. After Johnny Reese had answered him, he continued to flag, indicating urgency. Now, with legs atremble and knees aknock, he followed the train, at a walk, to where it stood. There was no more run in his legs just then. He advised the crew that they should flag their way back to Walhonding, the last station, and there get further instructions.

In the baggage car, fortunately, there was a roll of wire, which he borrowed. With a discarded spike for a hammer and the outside corner of the rail for a set chisel, he cut off appropriate lengths with which he would attempt a jury-rig repair of the downed lines. He had never done this before, but gumption told him that he should join the wire from a certain insulator on one pole to the wire from the corresponding insulator on the next. This turned out to be the way to do it.

Back at his office, Oscar gave Cambridge his report and an estimate of the extent of the slide. He was asked how close No. 909 had come to hitting this and he said, "One engine length." Thus, his heroic action became a division classic, and people stopped asking him how much manure a hopper car held.

The Distaff Branch

Craftswomen in the morse field were few and far between, especially on the railroad. Here they were at a disadvantage because of laws in several states that banned their working certain night hours. At the same time, the rules of seniority precluded their holding any but third trick, the night shift, in their beginning years. I was never to meet a woman operator personally, but those I listened to were quite as efficient as any man telegrapher.

One member of the distaff clan, after some two years of employment, received a postgraduate lesson in hand signals. She was on second trick at a cabin job, where she tended several ground switches. No interlocking here, and reverse movements through the plant were governed by hand signal.

A pusher engine, backing, had cut away from an eastbound freight on the fly. The operator's instructions were to cross the engine over and send it back west. She was duly stationed on the ground when the movement cleared her switches. The pusher, headed west, stood in the path of the eastbound General, No. 48, now closing in. Prompt action was called for.

The two switches of the sixty-foot-long crossover were secured in place by a lock rod, or plunger, the operating handle of which was located midway between the two. Much footwork was involved. The pusher engineer watched from his cab as the operator's lantern bobbed back and forth. At last she raised the lantern and swung it in a full-arm circle. In railroad sign language, this would commonly be interpreted as "back up and make it snappy." But this signal raised doubts in his mind. He supposed that he would cross over and head westward—the usual procedure. But if it was the case that one of the switches or the lock rod had proved inoperable, then maybe he was being signaled to back on to the next station, where he might get out of No. 48's path.

It was no time or place to guess, so he slid to the ground and approached her. "Why don't you move?" she asked sharply. "I gave you a signal to come on back."

"You gave me a backup signal," he said, "but my engine is headed west. You should have given a proceed signal."

She had, indeed, as she said, motioned him to "come hither," as she might motion another person to approach her.

The engineer hurriedly got back aboard and dug out of there in the westward direction. But before switches could be restored, the General's headlight stared at them from the home signal.

Tomorrow somebody would have to answer.

On the one occasion when I myself heard and watched a woman operator in action, I did this with fascination and admiration. Distance lends enchantment, it is said, and maybe this had something to do with it. It happened in Santa Fe's passenger station at Williams, Arizona, where my family and I awaited transportation up to Grand Canyon. I heard a morse wire at work in the office and was attracted to this as the farmhand is to the dinner bell. I stood near a ticket window and scanned the interior.

Several seated employees were at work with their backs to me. One, I knew, must be the morse operator, but I couldn't determine which until one stood up and began to detach copies of a train order just received and to affix these in a pair of order hoops—incidently, of the same style in use on my railroad. This operator was now recognizable as a young woman.

Now, through an east window, she watched the controlled approach of a westbound passenger train. With her right hand she appeared to operate a device that governed the aspect of a wayside home signal. At the proper moment she cleared this signal, grabbed the two hoops, and was out through two doors with the grace of a faun. I watched as she handed on the order exactly as I would have done. I thought of introducing myself, but she was busy and my wife was standing by.

The Trouble Shooter

I had been around a good while and had long learned to take nothing for granted on the job when, one night, this principle paid off.

By this time, virtually all passenger equipment had roller-bearing journals. These were not supposed to run hot, and they rarely did. Through long habit, however, I liked to study the wheels of all passing trains. I had so often been justified by spotting trouble in the making. In darkness, by eye, nose, or ear, I had pretty well learned to distinguish between hotbox, sticking brake, or sliding wheel.

I was out on my stoop one night giving passing inspection to the eastbound Liberty Limited, rolling by at fifty mph. The polished surface of main-track rail here reflected the blue-green of neighboring streetlights. When a train went along, this became a twinkling pattern. Beneath one of the Limited's trucks one twinkle—a mere eyewink—was out of character. It was a dull red. I watched the truck out of sight but saw no repetition.

I reported the train's passage but said nothing further. I

wanted to give the matter study. I had five minutes in which
to act or decide not to act before the Liberty left my block. I
studied the alternatives. Where the flash had occurred there
was no joint or frog from which a flange might have struck a
spark. I recalled what I had seen and was not willing to dis-
miss it as imaginary. The next several block stations in a row
were on the other side of the track, so the trouble, if any,
might not be spotted there. The next station ahead had a
remote-control switch and signal at the west end of its siding, where the Liberty could be stopped and sidetracked if
necessary. She was on time. A stop for a brief inspection
would not hurt her too much. And, of course, I had a rule
to fall back on. The rule said, "In case of doubt, the safe
course must be taken."

I told the dispatcher of what I had seen and of my conclusion. The Liberty was stopped at the remote-control station.
I answered the engineer's ring on the wayside phone and
told him that they should inspect the lead truck of the second car from the rear for a hotbox. The conductor was next
on the line a few minutes later. He said, in effect, "We've
got a hotbox and she's a dandy. I'm afraid to move the
thing. The journal box is red hot, so the journal itself is
probably white hot and soft. Head us for the siding and we'll
try to creep clear of the main. I'll have to set it off and
transfer about thirty passengers."

One of the very hard rollers of the bearing ensemble had
crushed and had chewed into the journal as would a
machine lathe. Next day the big hook came and put a new
truck under the sleeper.

No heroics were involved here . . . only a minute observation by one who had learned to expect the unexpected.

"Wheeling" was the name by which one engineer was

known, though none could tell you exactly why. If one raised the question, one got differing answers. The first three of his four initials were W. E. L. The W&LE (Wheeling and Lake Erie) Railroad crossed us at a couple of points, but he hadn't worked for that road. We had a Wheeling Division, but he hadn't worked there either. That he loved to "wheel," however, was known to all and denied by none. He was one of a lengthy roster of highly skilled passenger enginemen with enviable records, worthy emulators of Casey Jones of song.

Wheeling had piercing black eyes and a somewhat sharp nose, and these features rather led one to expect a matching flamboyant spirit. Thus, it was a surprise to hear him recount in explicit but soft language the story of his collision with a heavy truck at a grade crossing.

Wheeling was pulling Toledo-bound No. 117 with six or seven cars. He had just timed himself from milepost 95 to 96 and was doing seventy-five. He then glued his eye to Fairhope Interlocking's home signal until he passed under it, when his glance fell again to the track. Fifty yards ahead, a huge loaded coal truck was creeping onto his track at Ice House crossing.

Wheeling now did several things at once. He gave a futile yank on the whistle cord, pulled the main-brake valve around to a guessed-at five-pound reduction, opened the sanders, closed the throttle, then joined the fireman in a kneeling position behind the boiler.

There was no feeling of impact as the K-4 took the heavy truck square on. For an instant the skylight in the canopy was darkened as they passed under a cloud of flying coal. A half mile down the track the train ground to a stop. Wheeling leaned out the gangway for a look backward. Directly opposite him, on adjacent No. 4 track, the flagman of a standing freight looked up at him inquiringly. Wheeling pointed and yelled at him, "Look out!" and the flagman narrowly jumped out of the path of a pair of heavy dual wheels from the coal truck, following a true course between the rails of his track and bearing down on him at 25 mph.

The closest call I remember having was one evening when a westbound freight piled them up in my interlocking plant at Orrville. The first car to jump was twentieth back from the engine and this occurred about twenty car-lengths short of my tower. They pitched, they rolled, they tumbled and sparked. I took a few steps toward the ground, with the idea of retreat, but at that moment a boxcar on its side came skimming along atop the rails of the track nearest me, headed my way. I stopped, and the car stopped a few yards away.

Irene, on her way home from a local school meeting a short while later, encountered the wreck at a street crossing about a block from my tower. With great trepidation she headed for the tower, not knowing whether she would find it standing or me alive.

Two of the cars involved in the wreck were tanks, containing I knew not what. I notified the fire department and police of this fact. The town was cut in half and would be for some time. There was not much I could do personally but I did, without orders, call our Fletcher Richards and Lester Maston, two of our ablest section foremen, knowing their services would be needed immediately.

The most volatile commodity in the wrecked tank cars turned out to be a multithousand-gallon cargo of whiskey in one. This car suffered a ruptured valve on its underside and the precious stuff gushed from this at "forty dollars a minute," as Ken Yockey, my car inspector, put it. Ken labored valiantly to repair the leak, but he needed help, so I called out Lester Welty, who lived nearby, and together they *effectively* sealed it, as I knew they would. They were a pair of ingenious workmen. Before this was accomplished, however, several of the local citizenry had carted off free whiskey in everything that would hold whiskey, including hats and boots.

The two car inspectors, Ken and Lester, waded and knelt in the stuff as they worked. Ken was more than an hour late in starting his twenty-five-mile-drive home. His good wife was, of course, concerned at his tardiness and had slept fitfully, if at all. When Ken entered the house, he heard her feet hit the floor in an adjoining bedroom. She appeared in the doorway, and her greeting was, "I smell whiskey!"

A Place Called Millbrook

Millbrook was a notorious place. Everything happened there and new improbabilities occurred regularly. Geographically, it was and is a swamp of many hundreds of acres between Wooster and Shreve, with Killbuck Creek coursing through the middle. It harbored every species of wildlife—mammal, bird, and reptile—native to the region,including rattlesnakes.

A trackman mowing weeds with a scythe once came up onto the sixfoot dragging a three foot rattler with fangs embedded in his rubber boot heel. The operator at RK, near the swamp's western limit, sat in his outdoor facility one day and heard mice rustling amid a pile of papers on the floor at his feet, or so he thought. Then he recognized his mistake. It was the warning buzz of a rattler! Somehow, he dove out the door without pausing to reorder his clothes. On summer nights rattlers might be found stretched out along the base of rails, attracted there by the stored-up heat of the day past. The flagman always looked twice before bending down to attach caps to the railhead.

153

Millbrook was many things to many people. If you asked the train dispatcher's estimate of the place he would tell you it was a curse and an abomination, a perpetual headache that was going to shorten his days on earth. Despite its four main tracks, which extended nearly four miles from BR on the east to RK on the west, and with water pans on two of these, it was habitually blocked with trains in busy times. It was a coal and watering station for trains on all tracks. The mammoth through freights, especially those westbound, commonly cleaned fires here as it was forty-eight more miles to Crestline, the end of the line. Those eastbound stopped to attach pushers, if for no other reason.

Things were clogged up at Millbrook one afternoon when passenger trains 452 from the west and 113 from the east were destined to converge there. Only one alley was open, this No. 3, the westward passenger track. The matter was weighed in the dispatcher's office and it was decided that No. 452 would be given the preference, while No. 113 would be held at BR. This would be a move against the current of traffic, by train order and manual block indication. The orders were duly issued to the operators at BR and RK, repeated by them and completed.

Following this, the conductor of a standing freight on No. 4 track called the operator at RK from the coal dock to discuss a problem. The operator presently had to excuse himself from the telephone to go on the ground and hand on the "right of track" order to No. 452. He told the conductor of the freight to wait. As No. 452 passed him he counted her cars, as was his habit. He had learned that when she hauled more than six she would take coal at Millbrook, her engine having last coaled at Toledo. Today she hauled eight.

Then, incredibly, as he reentered his office he heard the operator at BR on the dispatcher's speaker reporting No. 113 as having passed him. In a matter-of-fact tone he explained his signal had been cleared for her at the time he had copied the orders and that he had forgotten to return it to stop. No. 113 and No. 452 were now on a four-mile collision course. The dispatcher began screaming for RK, while holding down his bell. The RK operator ignored this and plugged in his east block phone. The freight conductor was still on the line. The operator told him to get out on No. 3 track and give No. 113 the "washout," and told him the reason why.

A fine point to be appreciated here was this operator's having counted the cars on No. 452, and so knowing that she would stop at the coal dock. Thus, his ordering that No. 113 instead of No. 452 be flagged was the slim factor that narrowly averted tragedy. The operator at BR had failed to play his final ace, which would have been to flag the trainman at No. 113's rear.

He was relieved within the hour. He should never have been hired, although he had had some railroad experience. It was learned that he had a history of mental instability. He had been "scraped from the bottom of the barrel" in the World War II pinch for manpower.

One night an eastbound Blue Ribbon stopped at SN Smithville tower's home signal, where the engineer dropped off at the wayside phone. He had a startling report for the operator. Moments earlier, while the train was in motion, a young man had come sliding down the tender's coal pile. He had an urgent report and a plea to make. He, with a companion of his own age, had been deadheading on the flat afterdeck of the tender. When the engine had scooped water at Millbrook the tank had overflowed and flooded this deck. His friend, he thought, had been asleep and had reacted by rolling over the side. A train scooped water at 40 mph. The chance of anyone sustaining such a fall and living to tell about it was slim.

A pusher crew was started for Millbrook to look for him. They found him sitting on the end of a tie. When they approached, he said, "I'm sure glad you fellows stopped. I'm darn near froze." He could walk with assistance. He was helped aboard the engine. At Wooster station he was put in a waiting ambulance. A few hours later he died of internal injuries as doctors examined him.

The coal-dock tender's job at Millbrook was strenuous and physically exhausting. Small cars resembling coal-mine cars and holding some two tons were filled with coal from hopper cars and pushed by hand onto the trestle that spanned the four tracks. From there the coal was dumped into the tenders of engines standing below. This required the strength of two men. Sometimes they would be short-handed and a trackman would be pressed into service after his regular day's work. A mere boy served in this capacity one night. He was strong and willing for a couple of hours, then drowsiness and inertia overtook him and his bones wearied. He stretched out on the hard platform, with the inch-wide cracks between its planking, directly above No. 4 track. A huge freight hauler, the 1-1, which he had just helped to coal, was getting its train under motion a few yards away. Its stack had the diameter of a barrel and its exhaust the force of a howitzer. Its initial blasts were slow, measured and mighty. Presently one of these occurred directly beneath the recumbent lad. He was lifted bodily some two feet, and as abruptly dropped. He was then awake for another spell.

So many things happened in the region known as Millbrook; and not all of these could be accounted for, according to Bill Yockey, Sr., a lifelong resident of the area. Bill was a car inspector and a conscientious workman of the old friction-bearing and dope-bucket era.

Sometimes, if prodded with a question or two, Bill would talk about the swamp. He didn't say so, but listening to him one gathered that he had both a fondness and a respect for this wilderness—also that he knew more of its trails, its inhabitants, its dangers, and its rewards than most. He said that when a ground fog covered its vast acreage, muskrat houses sticking above the mist resembled a great hay meadow in July harvest.

His description of daybreak on a spring morning is memorable. It was, he said, one grand chorus of birdsong. It came from every direction and filled the air. It rose from the swamp and came out of the trees. The voices ranged from the honk of the biggest geese to the trill of the least warbler.

But, Bill would tell you, the swamp was never a place to be taken for granted. If one became careless, that was when he would be surprised, and this was no doubt part of the swamp's fascination.

Bill and his beloved hound, neither of them young any more, went coon hunting there one night. He probably could not recount the times they had done this before. Deep among the trees the old dog announced that it had struck a warm trail. Bill followed the general direction of the sound. It would be time to close in when the dog barked "treed." But, instead of this, the dog presently passed his master, belly to the ground and running his mightiest. He was in panic and paid no heed to Bill's call. He was definitely headed out of the woods. This he had never done before.

With an uneasy glance behind and with shotgun at the ready, Bill followed. A half mile off he found the dog whimpering beneath their car. When the door was opened he eagerly jumped in, and this he had not done before either. He was never the first to quit the hunt. Bill was sure of only one thing. The faithful old dog had not spooked without reason. But the reason he would never know for sure.

Ten months later, with early fall again at hand, a possible solution to the mystery was revealed. Going up Shreve hill, the flagman of a three-man pusher crew gazed off into the underbrush and saw a black bear, "tall as a man," he said, as it stood on hind legs and ate from a bush. The other crew members confirmed the story. Was it this bear, or one like it, that had frightened the old coon dog? Maybe yes, maybe no. One didn't jump to conclusions where the swamp was concerned.

Public Relations

The CA&C crossed us at Orrville and the Columbus to Cleveland morning passenger train did much work at our station. In addition to heavy platform work, she traded cars with two mainline trains. She was assisted in this work by two yard engines and two able car inspectors, Bill Yockey, Jr., and Charley Welch. If she was gotten out of town in forty minutes, it was a job well done.

During much of this work the town's main east-west artery was blocked, many motorists were inconvenienced regularly, the police commonly came around asking pointed questions.

One morning she was all coupled and ready to leave, except for one detail. The brakes were set up in full emergency and would not release. The car inspectors walked the train from head end to rear and back again. One boarded the engine and affronted the engineer by examining his brake valves and gauges. They parleyed. If there was nothing wrong outside, then there must be something wrong inside. They boarded the train, one at each end. Bill entered

159

a day coach filled with restless passengers, some of whom wondered aloud why the train didn't move. One of these was a comfortably seated man, who had found a unique place to hang his overcoat. He had pulled down the conductor's emergency brake cord (more accurately a chain), running the length of the car just above the windows, and hung the heavy coat over this. Bill's patience was now extremely thin. Instead of asking the man to remove the coat, he did it himself—with a pair of grimy hands.

I once received a bad press in the local paper. A huge freight of some 125 cars had crept to a slow stop in my plant, effectively dividing the town through its middle. This was bad news for several reasons: That the brakes had applied themselves gradually indicated a slow leak in the train line—the piping system which, together with the flexible hose between cars, carries compressed air from the engine to the last car. Unlike a clean break, which reveals its location by a continuing roar, the slow leak was often like hunting the needle in the haystack. The train must remain coupled and air constantly supplied by the engine or the leak might never be found.

I was busy with train orders as we prepared to reverse trains around the stalled one. At this point, a strange young man entered the tower, having ignored the No Visitors sign at the bottom of the stairs. He said he was a reporter. He asked why the train had stopped and how long I expected to hold it. My answer was short as I told him it had a broken train line and that I didn't know how long it might be here.

In the paper next day he intimated that the operator had given him a runaround by saying there was a break in the train line. "But," he wrote, "this reporter walked the entire train and there was no break in its line [of cars]."

Passing a message on the order hoop as the train rides through the station

More recently, in this vein, an elected city official was quoted in print as declaring in council, "Trains don't have to stop on our crossings for emergencies. They can stop a hundred yards back." This would be akin to ordering the descending parachutist to go on back, or perhaps telling the wind which way to blow.

A gap in communications, or terminology, exists here, of course. A train that stops because of an inadvertant application of the brakes is said to be "stopped in emergency." In almost all cases, the phrase is used to denote an air leak (great or small) in its train line, carrying seventy to ninety pounds of compressed air, generated by the engine. But such misunderstandings are probably inevitable.

Another War

Came December 11, 1941, and the sun again rose with an ominously red face. Two years earlier, Germany, once again with grandiose ambitions, had embarked on world conquest. Hitler, the psychopath, meant to succeed where Kaiser Wilhelm, the dreamer, had failed. He told his people they were a super race, and they bought this. The initial targets would once again be France and England. This time Germany would do an end run around the Maginot Line, once again trampling Belgium underfoot en route. Once again we would rally on a grand scale to the support and the supply of our former allies—again some two years before committing all our military might to the Allied cause.

The Japanese chose December 7, 1941, as an opportune time to jump on our backs at Pearl Harbor. But they reckoned without their host. President Roosevelt termed this "A day which will live in infamy" and everybody, but everybody agreed with him.

I think my thought was, "here we go again." On the railroad it was World War I all over, only more so. For me it was much more so, as I was now situated much nearer the center of the fire.

I had accumulated much experience in the interim, and here I was to employ it all. Second trick at Orrville was a notorious hot spot, even without a war. We were a block and interlocking station on the trunk line Eastern Division between New York and Chicago. We were a manual block and train order station on the single-track CA&C, which crossed us here. Daily we traded trains with this division, to and from Columbus to the south and Cleveland to the north. Occasionally we would learn by the grapevine that one of these was a munitions train from the Ravenna arsenal. Or, if the engineer in passing drew a finger across his throat and pointed back at his train, you nodded in understanding but spoke no word to anybody.

For the main line we had a pusher pool, which grew to twenty-seven three-man crews, manning fifteen L-1 engines at its height. Serving both divisions here were two H-10 yard engines.

A Record of Trains, which we called the block sheet, was to be maintained for both the CA&C and the Eastern Division. For the main line, this record had space for 200 entries, 100 east and 100 west. Around seven P.M. daily, I would cut a ten-inch piece from a new sheet and paste it on the bottom to hold the rest of the day's business up until midnight. I realize today that one of these would be a dandy memento, but I'm afraid none are available. They would also serve to convince some younger railroaders, who will not believe this story.

First- and third-trick operators here, both older than myself, were afforded levermen. No more were available. My boss suggested that I try to hire somebody, but the thought was appalling. To try, under these conditions, to break in somebody new to the railroad was mind boggling. I would slug it out, often reminding myself of how much better off I was than my countrymen who served at the front or on the sea.

Beloved Howard Hunter on first trick was permitted, by his own judgment, to work one hour over with me when conditions warranted. He often spent this hour recopying a supply of the standing train orders that adorned much of the table. When this was done we were supposed to go on the dispatcher's line and repeat what was rewritten. But this rule was generally ignored, as we hadn't the time for this, nor had the train dispatcher the time to listen. Howard might also ready my lanterns for use at dusk.

It was the rule rather than the exception to walk in on a jam at three P.M. and leave the place at 11 P.M. in the same condition. There was no time to eat. Frequently my pint of tepid coffee served as my only lunch until quitting time.

Once in great while we got a break. Westbound trains climbed a slight grade to reach the level of my interlocking plant. Heavily loaded engines would sometimes surmount this only to stall when the drivers spun as they crossed the CA&C diamond where its two-and-a-quarter-inch-wide flangeways made gaps in the rail. At ten o'clock one night this circumstance appeared to be once more in the making. A huge freight was laboring mightily while still many yards short of my home signal. Express train No. 99 followed closely. I made a couple of anxious trips to the doorway to listen. Then, to my mystified surprise, the tempo of the freight's exhaust commenced to pick up. Finally the rear end passed me at 10 mph. At the same time, the headlight of No. 99's K-4 stared at me from the home signal. Without cutting away from her train, she had coupled into the creeping freight and performed a noble job of pushing, while violating every rule of procedure ever written on the subject. I smiled to myself, perhaps for the first time that day, and said nothing to anyone.

It was at this time in our struggle and endless effort to keep trains moving that "unrealistic command" raised its ugly head in a dismaying manner. This took the form of an order from the superintendent, tacked on the wall one day, to the effect that an engine must no longer be given the fixed (home) signal to return to its train when said train was within interlocking limits.

In practice, this meant that the operator could no longer send an engine back to its train via the fixed signal. Instead, he would have to authorize each such individual movement by means of the official form C clearance card, duly filled out, signed, and personally delivered to the engineer who waited at the far end of the plant or beyond, depending on how many cars he had hold of.

In order to insure that this would be carried out, the signal department had that day, on orders, rigged the track circuits so that the electronic dwarf signals would not indicate in this circumstance.

The order was inane, asinine, pointless, and obstructive. Had it originated with an enemy agent, it would at least have made sense. It would affect operations here on all tricks, particularly on second and third, when there was an exchange of cars among several passenger and express trains with the aid of our two yard engines.

I formed an uncomplimentary mental picture of the author of this fatuity. He wore a white shirt, of course. His hands were also white and the nails polished. He was a relative of some high official. He had been to college, where he was highly trained in theory but abysmally neglected in practice. He probably had never done a day's work in his life, on or off the railroad. He didn't know a switch stand from a library table. He was desperately trying to justify his position and salary. He was harebrained.

When I had assimilated this order on reporting for work that day, I turned and scanned the bulletin board to see what, if any, other jobs might be up for bid. But this would be the cowardly approach, I decided. I would have to think of something else. Now I recalled some words of Lincoln's to the effect that the best way to get rid of an unpopular law is to enforce it to the letter. I would give this a try. A couple of safety rules now came to my aid. One of these forbade me to run on the tracks, and the other forbade me to hop a ride on engine or cars.

Westbound express train No. 99 would prove my best opportunity to apply the new ruling. This night she drove in some time after ten and spotted her working mail and express cars at the platform, already a half hour late. I don't remember ever before having rejoiced at this circumstance. Tonight, instead of picking up five minutes here, as she sometimes did, I would stick her for an additional twenty five—all within the law and the new rule.

Behind No. 99's third car would be two cars for Orrville; three outgoing cars would then be added in their place. A yard engine would proceed with this work after No. 99's head end had cut off and run clear of the plant. Thus, all told, there would be three reverse moves in the interlocking limits for which no fixed signal could be displayed.

I had made out the final form C, this one allowing No. 99's head end to return and couple up, when the Liberty was reported to me from a point five minutes to the west. I was required to be on station and in view when this train passed me, so I waited for it. When I reported the Liberty's passing to the dispatcher, he asked about 99. I told him I would have her out of town in about another fifteen minutes. He wanted to know what the delay was, and I spent another two minutes explaining this. He said, "Can't you open your window and give her a backup with your white light?" "Sorry," I reminded him. "The rule says a train must not proceed on a hand signal as against a fixed signal." He said no more, except to complain that he would now have to sidetrack No. 99 for the more important No. 15, and thus further delay the U.S. mail and the express, of which this train was composed. Next day, when I reported for work at 3:00 P.M., a man from the signal department was on hand to explain to me the workings of a bootleg arrangement that would nullify, or circumvent this new incongruity. Lincoln had been right.

Metamorphosis

World War II, our greatest of all national efforts, ended sometime in 1945. We have no memorable date to which we may point, such as November 11, 1918, or April 9, 1865. Possibly this was a portent of the many ways in which the status quo was due to change.

The brasspounder, after serving his fellowman well for roughly a hundred years, looked up and was shocked to note how low in the western sky was his sun. By the war's end our roster listed many block operators who did not telegraph. These had been ill received in the craft at first and were disparagingly treated at times. It was a professional jealousy of little merit.

Bill Given, red haired, Irish, and with the quick-flaring temper associated with his kind, was trying to converse with one of these on a noisy block fone (the common railroad spelling). He said to the fellow, "Come on the wire so I can understand you." The other replied, "You're out of luck, I don't telegraph." Bill shot to his feet as though he had sat on the cat. Raising a fist above his head, he said, *"I'm* out of luck, *he* don't telegraph!"

A nontelegrapher, having the unfortunate surname of Post, hired on a neighboring division. He immediately and widely became known and was addressed as "Fone Post." He remained only until he found more compatible work elsewhere.

We had supposed and expected that our railroads, after their monumental earnings during the four-year period of the war, would emerge again as a robust and stalwart private enterprise. Instead, it soon became evident that the winds were going to blow another way.

It was hard to accept that the railroads would prove to be another war casualty, and one of the greatest. Track, motive power, and rolling stock had taken a severe beating during the war. When the railroad sought to float large-scale loans for the purpose of rehabilitation, the lenders—and there were many of them—conspired to attach strings to the money and dictate how it might or might not be spent. Their approach was the retreat, the cutback, the minimal repair and replacement of plant—the "fast buck" in other words. They exhibited neither concern for nor appreciation of the proven vision of practical railroad people.

It was circa this time that a national epidemic of rail wrecks prompted the Interstate Commerce Commission to summon to Washington a whole bevy of railroad presidents, with the view of asking why. One of these, the president of a western road with office in Chicago, I have always thought spoke for the group at large said in just a dozen words, "Gentlemen, in my case it's the result of too many bankers railroading." I thought he should have been given a medal for speaking out.

It is in no way conceivable that the Allied cause would

have been victorious in either of the century's two great wars without the contribution of American and Canadian railroads—with an assist from A. Hitler in World War II, who expanded Germany's autobahns at the expense of her railroads.

Following World War II, our own highway-building program, which had lapsed during this period, once again got into high gear. Today our railroads that span and crisscross the nation are paralleled mile-for-mile by public highways. Had it been our deliberate purpose to sabotage the rails, we would have gone about it in just this way. The example of Adolph Hitler and his autobahns had passed completely over our heads.

It is inconceivable that, as of today, our railroads could repeat or even approximate their performances during the two great wars. If I could have the president's ear, I would like to emphasize this and argue further that some billions of his military budget might profitably be diverted to railroad rehabilitation. In doing so, a powerful intangible might be restored and profited by: that is, pride.

Let us remind ourselves further that railroads are privately owned, maintained, and operated—and publicly taxed; that instead of devouring a continuing river of public funds they are, or at least once were, the country's greatest *payer* of taxes.

Our railroads are down—victims of monumental miscalculation. But they have entirely too much going for them, including history, to be counted out. The pendulum at the end of its swing always starts back, and the ebb tide flows again.

Today there are many small but encouraging signs of resurgence. One of these is the ever-growing number of piggyback trailers that ride the railroad for much of their route. When piggybacking began, some thirty years ago, this trickle of freight was gratefully accepted as a small and unexpected bonus. Since then, the piggyback's speed, facility, and economy on the long haul have been ever more appreciated and patronized. Today, piggybacks make up an important percentage of rail freight. One of the more common piggyback cargoes has been the load of fresh fruits and vegetables from the west coast, each unit with its attached refrigerating unit. The latest addition, in significant and growing amount, is the United States mail—once again.

The railroads, I believe, are destined to reemerge as the prime mover of people and freight on land. Much less is to be said for this grandiose highway system of ours, solely reliant on oil, which the world will run out of ere long. As of today, our highway system deserves to rank among the seven wonders of the world. Tomorrow it may be looked upon as one of man's grand futilities, comparable to the Great Wall of China.

These observations are bolstered by the example of the "integrated coal train" that passes through our midst daily. The word *integrated* here connotes an innovation, this being that the cars of these trains remain ever coupled and move as a unit from Appalachian coal fields to destinations up north, then back again, following a schedule. Recently, I gave a running inspection to one of these trains, which was most revealing. It consisted of eighty-eight cars, all with roller-bearing journals. The load on each was symmetrically rounded up to the car's stenciled capacity, which was two hundred thousand pounds or one hundred tons. Its length was near four thousand feet, its speed about 35 mph. It was hauled by five diesel units and a crew of five (these, incidentally, immune to "highway hypnosis").

A little arithmetic told me that to shift the tonnage of this one train to public highways would require 352 trucks of twenty-five tons capacity each and, of course, that many drivers. The hourly wage cost here, added to a twenty-to-one differential in fuel cost per mile, plus again the cost of retiring the coal truck's multiwheeled cab and body at a cost of two thousand dollars, must surely tip the economic scale in favor of the rails.

As the cost of oil and oil products, plus that of highway maintenance, continues inevitably to spiral, more and more shippers the nation over will turn toward the rails with their proven economy and capability. And as the ever-rising cost of gasoline is added to the commuter's present problems of polluted air, parking, the chain cóllision, and the traffic jam, the needs and demands for mass transit are bound to increase. The railroads, already in possession of the foundations for such systems, will once again stand to profit from this commerce.

In the early 1950s the nation's railroads, with the exception of some minimal electrified miles, turned their backs on coal and joined the ravenous host of oil consumers, as the steam engine was replaced by the diesel. Thus did the railroads do their hefty bit to hasten the day when the wells must inevitably run dry. Today, twenty-five years later, such a changeover would not be accorded serious thought.

Some men arrived at my station in a truck one day. They brought with them saws, axes, and dynamite. When they left, our 120-foot-high coal dock, a landmark of many decades, lay on the ground. Its fall sent shock waves through the community and through the many onlookers. One of these, an oldster, walking away, said, "I hope they know what they're doing," and others of us echoed the thought. Several hundred pigeons, to whom the old dock had been home, present and ancestral, felt likewise as they circled the area till dusk in bewilderment.

Recently, a writer of keen insight set forth our problem in other words. "Our instinct," he said, "has ever been to advance: to advance where? Isn't it probable that we have already advanced to the brink, and that it is now time to retreat a bit in the direction of reality?"

Thus, the railroads will soon begin looking for a cheaper and more dependable fuel source. In doing so they are bound to rediscover coal—what else? They were founded on coal and on coal they grew to their greatest efficiency, public service, and profit.

However, the clock is never turned back, it is said. The new steam locomotive may not exhaust as the old ones did. It may be of the turbine type, supposed to exert a steady pressure on the drivers, and thus pull fewer drawbars, break fewer knuckles, and jerk fewer sleeping passengers awake. The coal may be pulverized or even liquefied and be blown into the firebox by the turn of a valve. This pulverized or liquefied product may be scooped from the track by the moving train, as water once was and could be again. The engineer, in a clean shirt and with no black under his nails, might not be recognized as such by those of my era.

Coal, of course, is also an irreplaceable resource, but many times more abundant than oil, and is found beneath

Don Sanders at home in Orrville, Ohio, in 1956

our feet, in abundance enough to keep us going for several more centuries, as far as we can estimate at present. On the farm, the old coal or wood-burning steam traction engine, which once pulled a six-bottom plow, threshed grain, filled silos, baled hay, and sawed wood is due to return to the scene. Even the faithful and patient horse—a historic friend of man who reproduces his own kind while helping to grow and harvest his own fuel—may be rediscovered.

In short, our next leap forward is apt to be a step backward in the direction of frugality and reality. In other words, we are coming to suspect that our bounty is not limitless.

We pride ourselves on being a first-rate world power, and indeed we are. We have proved as much on several occasions. But be assured, we cannot go on proving this by reference to past glories. It is my contention that viable railways, rather than roadways, will assure our position for some generations to come.

Pulling the Pin

On the railroad one doesn't retire from the service, he "pulls the pin." This is what occurs at the end of a run when the coupling pin is lifted and the engine put away in the roundhouse.

So it was that, at 11 P.M. on a night near the end of December 1965, I pulled the pin. It had been a long run, and I was about as anxious to quit as I had been to start out fifty years earlier. The railroad had become such a different place on which to work. I left a few personal belongings in a drawer, but I salvaged my agate-pointed stylus, which I had carried about for so many years.

A few weeks later my recent boss phoned me at home to suggest that Irene and I come to the local Manhattan Restaurant the evening of January 28 for a little dinner. This last division operator under whom I had worked was Clem Andrews. He was also a brasspounder of the first order, and we had understood each other. He and his gracious wife came down from Cleveland for the occasion. Some two dozen others, mostly old-timers, also came.

Pennsylvania Railroad hat

Fifty-year service pin

The dinner was featured by much laughter and reminiscence, and that is a nice way to remember it. Clem brought me a present and affixed it to my lapel. Nothing he might have chosen could have pleased me more. It was the official gold fifty-year retirement pin of the PRR. Etched on the back are my name and years of service. On the front, in bold relief, is a facsimile of the front end of the glamorous K-4, identified by her modified cowcatcher and keystone number plate, which latter she always wore so proudly at the front of her boilerhead.

I continue to live and relive this memorable evening.

Epilogue

According to Scripture, it is the "good and faithful servant" who wins immortality. Unquestionably, the railroads have proved good and faithful servants here on earth. What I am getting at is that if people are to be resurrected, why not things? Why not railroads? Fanciful thinking, maybe—but who knows?

THE PENNSYLVANIA RAILROAD COMPANY

This Certifies that Donald G. Sanders
Block Operator — Central Region
has been relieved of Active Duty, after 50 *years of Service,*
and that his name is enrolled on

THE ROLL OF HONOR.

Philadelphia, the 1st day of January 1966

President

Retirement certificate

Appendix:
The Morse Code

A	.‑		S	...
B	‑...		T	‑
C	...‑		U	..‑
D	‑..		V	...‑
E	.		W	.‑‑
F	.‑‑.		X	.‑..
G	‑‑.		Y	....
H	....		Z	.... .
I	..		1	.‑‑.
J	‑.‑.		2	..‑..
K	‑.‑		3	...‑.
L	———		4	.....
M	‑‑		5	‑‑‑
N	‑.		6	......
O	..		7	‑‑..
P	.....		8	‑....
Q	..‑.		9	‑... .
R	. ..		0	———

period	·· −− ··
comma	aa
dash	dx
colon	ko
semicolon	sc
question mark	dn
opening quotation	qn
closing quotation	qj
first bracket	pn
second bracket	py
(the pn and py above also denote first and second parentheses)	
dollar sign	sx
exclamation mark	−−− ·
one half	1e2
one third	1e3
etc.	

Glossary

AGENT–OPERATOR. The station agent who also telegraphs.

AUTOMATIC BLOCK. The main track between wayside signals.

BACKUP SIGNAL. Hand, flag, or lantern swung in a circle.

BIGHOLE. Emergency application of the air brakes.

BIG HOOK. The wreck train.

BLOCK OPERATOR. The employee in charge of a block station.

BLOCK SHEET. The block station's daily record of train movements—midnight to midnight.

BLOCK WIRE. The telegraph line between stations.

BLUE RIBBON FLEET. Posh passenger trains.

BRASSPOUNDER. The experienced telegrapher.

BUG. A patented high-speed telegraph key.

CLAMSHELL. Power-operated dipper.

CLIMBER. The telegraph lineman.

CROSSOVER. Rail arrangement between parallel tracks for moving trains from one track to another.

CROWN SHEET. The boiler section immediately above the fire box.

CRUMMY. The caboose.

DEADHEADING. Off-duty employees riding the trains.

DEAD KEY. The closed telegraph key used for practice by the beginner.

DECORATE. To ride the tops of cars, or freight trains.

DOPE BUCKET. A bucket of waste and heavy black oil used to oil the old friction-bearing car wheels or axles.

ELECTROMAGNETIC TELEGRAPH. Samuel F. B. Morse's name for his invention.

FIREBOX. Where coal was burned to heat the boiler.

FLAGMAN. The trainman protecting the standing train's rear.

FOREIGN CAR. One belonging to another railroad.

GANDY DANCER. Pick and shovel artist, paddy—the track repairman.

GONDS OR GONDOLAS. Low-sided open-top cars.

GREASE MONKEY. The car repairman.

GROUNDING. Shorting out the telegraph line for testing purposes.

HAM. The beginning telegrapher.

HANDCAR. Trackmens' hand-operated transportation on the rails.

HIGH IRON. The main track.

HIGH WHEELER. The passenger locomotive.

HOGHEAD. The engineer.

HORSELESS CARRIAGE. Baggage or express hand truck.

HOT BOX. The overheated journal.

INTERLOCKING PLANT. Station from which switches, derails, and fixed signals are operated.

LEVERMAN. Employee of an interlocking plant.

LINEMAN. Telegraph repairman and maintainer.

LINK AND PIN. Hand operated link and pin coupled cars together before the invention of the automatic coupler.

MAIN STEM. The main track.

MANUAL bLOCK. The main track between block stations.

MARKERS. Lights, or flags, denoting a train's rear end.

MILL The typewriter.

OP. Wire man, morse man, or telegrapher.

OPEN AIR MINER. The coal dock attendants.

PADDY. Section hand, or track repairman.

PHILLIPS CODE. An abbreviated dictionary of the English language.

PRACTICE SET. The beginning telegrapher's instruments.

PULLING THE PIN. Retiring from the service.

PULLMAN. Leased passenger equipment having both seats and sleeping berths.

RAILHEAD. The top part of the rail.

REEFER. A refrigerator car.

RIGHT-OF-WAY. Railroad property.

ROLLER-BEARING JOURNALS. These have now largely replaced the old friction type on car axles.

ROUNDHOUSE. Where the engine goes for repairs and other attention.

SANDERS. These piped sand from the sand dome atop the boiler to the rails, to maintain traction.

SANTA CLAUS. The pay car.

SEMAPHORE BLADES. The movable arms atop a signal mast.

SIDEWINDER. Patented telegraph key—not standard.

SIGNAL MAST. A pole supporting fixed signals at its top.

SINES. The individual letters of stations, or of telegraphers.

SIXFOOT. A manicured area of that width, bordering the main track.

SMOKEY. The fireman.

SPEEDER. An employee's three-wheel railroad handcar.

SPIKE MAUL. A sledge for driving spikes.

Spotter. A railroad official watching you.

Switchback. A zigzag arrangement of track for surmounting a hill. It lengthens the distance but lowers the rate of climb.

Switch key. It unlocks the ground switch, or derail.

Switch lamp. A lamp on a standard that may have a red, green, yellow, or purple lens to indicate a switch's or a derail's position after dark.

Switch point. The end of a tapered rail.

System car. One belonging to your own railroad.

Tamping pick. A tool used to shore up the low joint.

Telegraph table. The telegraph operator's desk.

Toad. Hand operated derail.

Trackwalker. He patroled the main line at night.

Trainline. Pipe and hose system that carried compressed air from the engine throughout the train to operate it's brakes.

Trick. An eight-hour segment of the twenty-four-hour day.

Trunkline. The cross-country, high-speed railroad.

Varnished cars. Passenger equipment.

Washout. Emergency hand-stop signal.

Water boy. He carried drinking water to the trackmen.

White collar. An official.

Work train. One equipped with ditching and ballasting tools and material.

Index